Repurpose Your Career
A Practical Guide for the 2nd Half of Life

Third Edition

Marc Miller
With
Susan Lahey

Repurpose Your Career
A Practical Guide for the 2nd Half of Life

ISBN-13: 978-0-9887005-5-0

PRAISE FOR
REPURPOSE YOUR CAREER

I always enjoy talking to Marc Miller for insights and stories about finding meaningful work in the second half of life. Now you can read his thoughts on the topic drawn from years of consulting with clients, as well as his own experiences. The information in each chapter is practical, with helpful action steps. But, as he reminds us, learning new skills and meeting new people should also be fun. Experienced workers still have enormous contributions to make to our society and economy.

Chris Farrell, author of *Purpose and a Paycheck*

Marc's insights into our late-career challenges are profound. For anyone navigating this new and uncertain life stage, his book provides a reassuring and empowering message.

John Tarnoff, career coach and author, *Boomer Reinvention*

The updated version of *Repurpose Your Career* offers a roadmap to finding meaningful work during the second half of life. Written by celebrated career coach Marc Miller, it is chock-full of proven strategies, relatable stories and actionable advice tailored to the unique needs of people over 50. If you want to make your next act your best act, start reading this book now.

Nancy Collamer, Semi-Retirement Expert and Founder of MyLifestyleCareer.com

I love this book. Marc points out that as we get older it becomes harder to "pretend to be something other than ourselves at work. Amen. The chapter about being a square peg in a round hole will resonate with many readers. Marc shows us how to live in our own unique "square hole" when we repurpose our career. I live by the mantra "make age 50 to 75 the best years of my life" - and you can't do that if your career ladder is against the wrong wall."

Thom Singer, Speaker and host of the "Cool Things Entrepreneurs Do" podcast

As usual, Marc Miller provides excellent advice on today's requirements for a successful job search and career, focused on helping those of us over 50 cope with all the changes happening. Marc describes how the whole work environment has shifted dramatically with the increasingly rapid growth in the use of technology – for example, how some older industries (and jobs) are disappearing while new industries (and jobs) are developing. In this latest edition, Marc describes how to recognize, adapt, and overcome the new barriers to continuing your career and your income.

Susan P. Joyce, owner of Job - Hunt.org

Attention job seekers! Whether you are relaunching your career, transitioning to a new one or just starting out in the work world, Marc Miller focuses on actionable strategies for the most important and difficult parts of the job search. Read carefully and benefit immediately from his expert advice!

Carol Fishman Cohen, Co-founder, iRelaunch

TABLE OF CONTENTS

INTRODUCTION

The first edition of Repurpose Your Career was published in January of 2013, when many Baby Boomers were still experiencing the devastating effects from the great recession. This is on top of the hits that many took from the dot com bust and more than a dozen years of abysmal returns in our retirement accounts. Retirement was progressively looking like something that was not going to happen.

Things looked pretty bleak, but we knew we had to pick ourselves up and go back to work.

By the time Susan and I started working on the second edition, a lot of things had changed.

- Many had gone back to work, but with a different perspective. They started to realize that their chosen career paths were not right for them.
- Social media had become pervasive in our society and the changes it was making were not all good.
- Automation was creeping even faster into the workplace.
- A younger demographic, Gen Xers, started to question their career choices

Therefore, we renamed the book to Repurpose Your Career – A Practical Guide for the 2nd Half of Life.

Now in 2019, the economy is humming along and everyone who wants a job should have a job. The numbers tell us that everything is looking up but those of us in the 2nd half of life know that is not true.

Many of us will now work into our 70s or beyond. Many are accepting the fact that being a full-time employee is not the only choice.

Automation, AI, and robotics have become workplace realities and creative destruction continues to accelerate. If we want to stay active and engaged, we had better embrace the changes.

This third edition is about how we embrace that change and make ourselves better.

We have removed some chapters on job search and other tactical subjects, but those will still be available in the Repurpose Your Career Resource Center at Careerpivot.com/RYC-Resources/

There is a paid membership community where you can find help in implementing the changes discussed in this book. Learn about the Career Pivot Community at Careerpivot.com/Community.

HOW TO USE THIS BOOK

This is not the type of book that should be read, cover-to-cover in a sitting. You probably could read the whole thing in a few hours, but then you wouldn't get the most out of it.

Every chapter has specific insights that I hope will spur specific reflections and actions. I hope you read a chapter at a time, put the book down, reflect back on your career, execute on the action steps, and then move on to the next chapter. I encourage you to take notes, highlight sections and move through the book thoughtfully. Those of us in the 2nd half of life have volumes of experience to draw upon, ponder and learn from. Take the time to reflect back upon those experiences.

To really get the most out of this book could take weeks or months. You might even want to read it several times.

At the end of each chapter is a set of action steps. There will be a link to the Repurpose Your Career Resource Center, where you will find copies of the action steps in Microsoft Word format along with a variety of worksheets and other resources to assist you in your journey.

You will be asked for your e-mail to gain access to the resource center.

Check out the accompanying online Career Pivot Community at CareerPivot.com/Community.

In other words, it's great if you get insights from reading this book, but you'll get so much more if you use it as a tool to inspire reflection, action and growth.

TIME FOR RETIREMENT? NOPE.
TIME FOR REINVENTION

Finally, we're at full employment! As of the writing of this book, unemployment rates are below four percent. Everybody who wants a job has one, right? Well, no, not exactly. I mean, that's what most of the data says. But it doesn't *feel* true. The data seems to be leaving something out.

The AARP Public Policy Employment Data Digest shows that most people over 55 who want to be employed are. In fact, the unemployment rate for this age group was a little over three percent as of February 2019. Unemployment numbers are based on the number of civilians who are not employed by an institution and are either working or looking for work. But I go to a fair number of groups for job seekers, and the faces I see there tend to be, well, old. Some of that is because these people have been unemployed for a long time. Being unemployed for more than 26 weeks is a real drag on your health and can make you look old. About 22 percent of unemployed people have been unemployed that long, according to Bureau of Labor Statistics. But the other reason they look old is that more than a third of long-term unemployed people are over 55. Possibly it's wiser to use the data from the U6, an unemployment metric that takes into account underemployed, discouraged and marginally affected workers. If you count those people, the unemployment rate was actually seven percent as of July 2019—more than twice the other projections.

In Austin, Texas, where I live part time, the unemployment rate is below three percent—unless you're over 50. If you're over 50 it's above 12 percent. Back in 2015, *The Atlantic* published the article "Where Not to Be Old and Jobless," which listed Austin as the fourth worst place to be old and unemployed, behind San Jose, California; El Paso, Texas; and New Haven, Connecticut.

Research by the AARP reveals that more than 10 million people over 50 live in poverty and more than 37 million are just "one life event away" from poverty. This is especially a risk for older women. So, the organization has funded a program at Austin Community College called Back to Work 50+. It's a great thing that the AARP has funded this program. But here's the question: If we're at full employment, why do we need a special program for employing people over 50?

Why are so many people in this age group unsuccessfully looking for work?

The AARP statistics don't include retired people, by the way. While I do know some people who have successfully retired before age 65, most of them were government employees, or they retired because either their health or their spouse's health was poor. I also know people who gave up looking for jobs and just started taking Social Security early. Forty percent of people who initiate Social Security do so at the age of 62, the earliest age when you can get your Social Security benefits. Only seven percent wait to take Social Security until the maximum age of 70. This is a real problem, because if you take Social Security before your full retirement, you lose a lot. If you were born in 1960 and take retirement at 62, you lose 30 percent. On the other hand, if you were born in 1960 and you wait to take your full benefit until after you turn 70, you gain 24 percent.

So back to the question: Why are so many people over 55 unemployed and looking, compared to the rest of the population? Is it ageism? Do they lack the skills for today's workplace? Or is it something else?

The answer is yes.

AGEISM IS ALIVE AND WELL, BUT....

Ageism is real, and it's thriving in places like Austin, where a lot of the economy revolves around tech startups. If your skills are up to date, you have a solid work history, you're physically fit, you dress like you know what year it is, and you're not looking or acting old—except for some wrinkles and gray hair—and they still don't hire you because the "culture" is younger, that's age discrimination.

I have lots of examples from the Career Pivot Online Community where members have acquired skills in the latest programming technologies and data science and still cannot get hiring managers to speak with them. Hiring managers do not want to invest in the careers of people in the second half of life. The reason I've heard for this is, "The applicants do not have enough career runway."

Considering that most people change jobs every four to five years, and Millennials change jobs every two years or so, should employers be worried about these older workers' career runway? When we are at full employment, should we be worried about having enough career runway? That is an example of ageism.

But ageism isn't always the culprit. Sometimes people claim ageism when the truth is they have let themselves and their skills go to seed. A lot of older people try to get by without learning new skills, hoping to coast toward retirement. But in this rapidly changing environment driven by creative destruction, your career track may evaporate long before you're ready to retire. In such cases, your experience may not help you get the next job.

Think of it like trading in a car. When I traded in my 2003 Honda Element, it didn't have GPS or Bluetooth. It didn't have heated seats or a hybrid engine. Plus, it had some wear and tear. It looked like a car that had been on some road trips. Because of that, the dealership offered me a much lower price than they charged me for my new car. They discriminated against my Honda Element!

If you haven't bothered to update your skills, including everything from learning the current vernacular to using newer apps or collaboration software, you're keeping yourself out of the workforce. If you tend to gripe about having to learn new technologies or communication channels, or find yourself repeating stereotyped condemnations against Millennials, you're keeping yourself out of the workforce.

There is no question that a skills mismatch exists in the employment market. Creative destruction is accelerating through many industries, eliminating positions of people who honed their skills over decades. I've had clients whose whole career worlds disappeared in under five years.

So, what do you do? Keeping your skills up is crucial, but it's not enough to keep you employed. You need to be creative. You need to be agile. You need to be ready to reinvent yourself every few years to match what the market needs.

Forget cruise control. It's time to get a manual transmission and learn how to use it.

ADAPT OR BE LEFT BEHIND

Marti Konstant, author of *Activate Your Agile Career: How Responding to Change Will Inspire Your Life's Work* said it best: *adapt or be left behind.*

You can plan for a future that will be significantly different from today, or you can *be left behind.*

It is a choice! Many of us will want, or need, to work into our 70s. Working in our 70s will not look like working in our 50s. It will most likely be a combination of different types of jobs: multiple part-time jobs, starting a side gig, finding different ways to make money.

Many of us don't think like that. We were raised to be employees. We believed that finding a job was the quickest, surest way to security. We'd get in there and stay until we got our gold watch. Today, that ain't happening. For one thing, it will be tough to get anyone to hire someone in their 60s. But beyond that, these days even the companies can't promise they'll be around in five years.

Your employer isn't going to save your butt. You have to get creative.

Look at all the jobs that used to be done by people that are now done by robots. Most service jobs, for example, can be done by robots; and many people prefer dealing with self-service options over interacting with other humans. Among the professions that experts predict are going to be replaced by machines are respiratory therapy techs, computer operators, legal secretaries, and everybody at the post office. Consider how Uber transformed the taxi industry, how Airbnb transformed the hotel industry, and how the iPhone has transformed, well, everything since it was released in 2007.

Among the things we can now do on our smart phones:

- Banking

- Sending messages

- Watching and making videos

- Learning languages

- Listening to music

- Scheduling

- Budgeting

- Shopping

- Booking a hotel

- Booking a flight

- Finding a date

- Joining a meeting

- Getting directions

- Paying for things

And that's just for starters.

 Because many of the menial tasks have been taken off the table, what remains is often more meaningful. And meaning is a key to finding your happy place when it comes to work. Whatever path you take might disappear in the future, so you can't get hung up on the path. You have to think in terms of constant evolution. Many members of the Career Pivot online community are taking bold actions to be ready for the change. One is Mike Martin, a drone pilot instructor whose story you will learn about later in the book. When Mike started his journey, there was no such thing as a drone pilot instructor.

Camille Knight is a logical creative. She grew up as a dancer and singer. Her first degree was in music; then she went back and got a degree in business. She worked in HR, got spit out of Whole Foods, and reinvented herself as a business analyst. She discovered Tableau software that lets her build beautiful dashboards that tell stories. For the first time in her life, she gets to marry both sides of her brain.

I had a client who said he wanted to be a data scientist. I said, "No, you don't want to be a data scientist. You want to do scrap analysis for a manufacturer. It's not enough to just have a skill. You have to find a company's pain point. You have to solve a problem."

We are at an inflection point. You can no longer acquire a skill and be fitted into a job. Things change too fast. If you want to continue to be relevant, you must adapt to the speed of change. You have to find tasks and skills that are meaningful to you and adaptable to new technologies and cultural paradigms—or be left behind.

BE THE MENTOR YOU WANT TO SEE IN THE WORLD

Betty White said Facebook wouldn't do her any good in terms of helping her reconnect with old friends. "At my age," she said, "if I want to reconnect with old friends, I need a Ouija board."

It's a weird paradigm shift, getting older. We used to have mentors who could tell us what to do. Chances are, those mentors are retired now. There are no coattails for us to ride anymore. At this

11

stage, we *are* the coattails. Much of our network might be gone. We must forge the path ourselves.

Part of that is taking up the mantle and becoming mentors to younger people. Millennials and GenZ want mentors to help them evaluate how they're doing. As one Millennial wrote on the Millennial-oriented website The Muse, they've been conditioned to seek feedback and advice. So, yeah, they want that in their careers, preferably from someone who won't tell them they're entitled, lazy snowflakes.

In turn, they can help you tap into areas of the work world that might seem foreign to you, like the fact that there's a website called The Muse, or how to use Instagram to grow your business.

I know one freelance writer who meets with her mentees frequently for happy hour. They have helped her find work in markets where she would never have thought to look. In turn, she helps them with strategies for dealing with difficult clients, insights about networking, tactics for time management, and reassurance that being an adult isn't as scary as it looks.

We've entered a new dimension when it comes to work. It's more focused on continually developing yourself rather than sliding into position as a cog. The idea of just getting "old, tired, and set in your ways" is a recipe for obsolescence. And that's a good thing. Scientists have found that if we treat them right, our brains can learn and adapt right up to death. Now we just have to rethink the second half of life to stay vibrant, connected, and contributing.

This should be fun. _New Focus_ (adapt)

Trace - how can I evolve w/in this company?

? PM / Field Mgr / Management
? New Con cross training
? ~~other~~ Vendor mgmt / development
? ~~Cont'd learning Opps~~
? Continuing education
  - HVAC certs
  - Universal EPA cert.
  - OSHA ~~renewal~~
  - Power Bi

? What is AHM pain point? How can I be in a better position to help resolve?

ACTION STEPS

✓ Make a list of all the things you can think of that have changed in the way you function, and the way your industry functions, since you started your career.

✓ Make a list of what has stayed the same.

✓ Write down how your skill set might still work, or be tweaked, to meet the changes rushing toward you and what else you need to learn.

For additional resources, check out the Repurpose Your Career Resource Center at CareerPivot.com/RYC-Resources

14

YOUR FIRST STEPS TOWARD
YOUR NEW LIFE

I was on my way to China, standing in line to board the plane, when the question that had been picking at the back of my mind sprung up in front of me, huge and fully formed: What are you DOING?

Less than a year before, I had survived a nearly fatal bicycle accident. My bike hit the car—head on. Our combined speeds were 50 miles an hour. The car was totaled, and I should have been. But miraculously, though I spent five days in a trauma center, I recovered fully. At those speeds, there is a 10 percent chance of survival.

I was alive. The one life I get, that I know of. And I was once again getting on a plane to go somewhere I didn't care to go, to teach people how to design leading edge routers and switches that wouldn't change the world. I had been given a second chance at life; what was I doing with it?

I did take that trip and several others after it. (Sorry — there's no dramatic running-off-the-tarmac scene.) But that moment launched me on a journey to create a life I believed in. It took years, painful mistakes, and several course corrections. In fact, I don't think I'll ever be done learning and changing. But one thing I discovered while trying to find a good path for my life was that I was not alone — far from it.

When I shared the steps I was taking to change my life, friends and acquaintances looked at me with an expression of skepticism that tried to mask a mixture of longing and fear. They wanted to change their lives, too. How had I done it? Was it possible for them?

REINVENTION REQUIRES STRATEGY

I am a data guy who worked over 20 years for IBM and has years of experience training and teaching. I like systems. I like finding the most efficient and effective way of doing things. And I've learned that the most realistic approach to change is gradual, a series of steps to get you to your goal. Career change is not different. It's a series of pivots in the direction you want to move. That's why I called it a Career Pivot.

While making my own changes, and working with others on theirs, I've developed a pretty solid system. But if it's going to succeed for you, you will need to be really honest with yourself about where you are right now.

You should ask yourself:

- What is your skill set?

- When you make this change, will your family be behind you? Do you have a support system?

- How is your health? This will impact what kind of career you can consider.

- What is your financial situation and what future financial needs can you anticipate?

- How do you feel about change?

- Are you ready to give this process whatever is required to get it done?

The last one is important. Picking a new direction for your life requires traveling uncomfortable new territory.

And here's another question: Are you in your right mind? I'm not asking whether you're crazy. But all of us have a positive, sage brain and a negative brain. If you're thinking in terms of running away from your job or your life, chances are you're in your negative brain. Your negative brain tends to bring a whole lot of baggage to the process that you don't need. Your negative brain tells you how ill-equipped you are for what you want, how hopeless it all is, how unfriendly other people are being. It's a real downer.

My client Lisa was laid off and very upset about it. She was experiencing a lot of stress, anxiety, and anger. I don't know if it's energy, pheromones, or subtle clues, but when we're stressed like that, we repel people. Nobody wants to be around it. If Lisa had gone looking for a job in that condition, she would likely have been really unsuccessful, which would have made things even more discouraging for her.

Instead, I taught her a technique I learned from the book *Positive Intelligence* by Shirzad Chamine. It talks about naming your judges. Research shows that 70 percent of our self-talk is negative. But it helps a lot to *name* the negative voices — your judges — who are talking to you. One person, for example, named their judge Darth Vader. Lisa named hers Stresszilla. If you recognize your judges as being intruders on your thought process instead of part of your thought process, it helps you to turn them off.

Instead of looking for a job right away, Lisa took several months to nurture herself and recover from the shock. Then when she was ready to apply, everything — from her interview answers to her body language — communicated a much healthier message.

But you also need to ascertain whether you're running away from something or running toward something. This book will help you figure that out. If you're running away from something, you need to reframe your thinking so that you're running toward something. If you don't, it's a pretty safe bet you'll wind up in a mess very similar to the one you're currently trying to escape. For example, don't think in terms of escaping your controlling boss, think of looking for a company with a culture of autonomy and empowerment. Instead of trying to get out of a corporate environment, seek a job with minimal hierarchy, a focus on outcomes instead of processes, and a more close-knit team.

For this journey, you will need to embark on a lot of introspection: Who are you? How did you get here? Without this step, you might as well not bother, because you're likely to pedal hard to wind up in the same position you're in now.

You will have to stop being the expert with 20 years' experience and become the novice, asking for help. You may have to take courses, become smart about social media sites like LinkedIn and adjust your idea of what "the good life" is. If any of that sounds like a deal breaker, this may not be the moment for you to take the plunge.

But if it is the moment, I've got the tools to help you on your Career Pivot. Read on.

ACTION STEPS

✓ Take stock of where you are in your relationship, financial, health, and other aspects of your life. Write down what about this moment makes it good, or not so good, for a career pivot.

✓ Write down what you might be running away from and reframe those situations to be something you're running to.

✓ Assess whether you're in a good place to start a career pivot journey or what you need to do before you begin.

For additional resources, check out the Repurpose Your Career Resource Center at CareerPivot.com/RYC-Resources.

WHEN THE CLOUDS PART: MOMENTS OF CLARITY

Sam was in his late 50s in 2014, when he got laid off for the second time in five years. He'd been fanatical about saving for retirement. And here he was again, on the hunt for a job. It was fall. There was little use in job hunting during the holidays. So, he went on a walkabout.

A walkabout is a ritual practiced by aboriginal tribes of Australia. They send 13-year-old boys out into the wilderness to follow the trails their ancestors took. It's a rite of passage to see if they can survive on their own. Sam's walkabout was a little different. He got a rail pass and decided to head west and see the country.

He slept on friends' couches. He slept in his car. Once he even spent the night, illegally, on a park bench. He was gone for a month. And while he was away, he had an epiphany. He'd always been worried about having enough money for the lifestyle he expected to live in retirement. But now he didn't feel like he needed it. All he really needed was good food, good coffee, a place to sleep and a place to work out.

This was Sam's moment of clarity.

Moments of clarity are those times when the assorted junk that plagues your mind—your annoying co-worker, your extra 15 pounds, the ugly tile in your bathroom, or your battle over which one of you gets a new car—suddenly vanishes in the face of something life-altering. It might be that your child is sick, or your spouse, or you. It might be a death in the family, a divorce, a layoff, or a natural disaster. It might even be good news, like an inheritance or an opportunity.

Or a walkabout.

Whatever it is, it turns your perspective upside down. Suddenly the way you were living doesn't make sense. "Why did I ever think that ugly tile was important?" you think to yourself. "Why did I spend so many sleepless nights over that argument? Why didn't I pursue my dreams? How did I not see the truth before?"

A moment of clarity may or may not touch on your career. But if it does, it reveals truths you've been ignoring or deliberately hiding from yourself.

You might realize that your parents pushed you into a career you didn't want, or that the company you work for has institutional barriers that will never let you succeed. You might see that you always wind up with narcissistic bosses, and begin to unpack the reasons why. You might realize you habitually undermine yourself, selling yourself short to more powerful colleagues. Or you might see that you value freedom over money.

Because of a dramatic — if temporary — change in circumstances, nothing looks the same as it did yesterday. The filters that prevented you from seeing things as they are have fallen, giving you an opportunity to learn something about yourself.

At those times you learn what is really important to you.

But those filters go back up quickly. The moment passes, and, next thing you know, the bathroom tile is bugging you again. If you don't act in that moment of clarity, or set a change in place, you'll go on as you were with a nagging sense of missed opportunity.

I am happy to say I have acted in a moment of clarity many times and was always better for it.

MY MOMENTS OF CLARITY

MY OWN WALKABOUT

When I was in my 20s, working for IBM, I took two weeks' vacation and two weeks without pay. I went to Colorado, Utah, and Arizona. It took me a few days to begin decompressing and realize how stressed I was. It took more days until I got to the point where I couldn't remember what day it was. By the time I came back, having spent only $500, I realized I could live on a lot less money than I thought I needed. I also was a changed person. That was when I met my wife, Lotus. If I had been the anxious wreck I was when I left, I don't know that our first encounter would have led to the 30-year marriage we've enjoyed.

THE DAY MY SON WAS BORN

The following several years were amazing.

We all know what sponges our children are. They pick up and mimic our behaviors, mannerisms, and languages. My son mirrored so many of my behaviors, both good and bad. He has taught me more about myself than I have learned from anyone else in my life.

I made changes that included how I ate (too fast), how much alcohol I drank, the type of language I used. I had to get rid of those four-letter words, and the need to care for him forced me to get to bed and rise on a regular basis. All of these made me a better and healthier individual and father.

WHEN I HURT MY BACK

In December 1992, I ruptured the L4/L5 discs in my lower back. I either had to get an operation or take three months off on disability to recover. I chose to take the time off. I'd always overloaded myself with projects, but now I was forced to relax.

In the process, I discovered peace. All my previous stress seemed so unnecessary in light of this revelation of being calm. Simple things became delightful. When I went back to work at IBM, the company was near bankruptcy and my stressed-out colleagues were panicked about being unable to afford their bloated lifestyles. But I saw clearly that I didn't want to swap my newfound peace for this anxiety again. I was willing to make whatever changes necessary to my career and lifestyle to preserve my contentment.

MY BICYCLE ACCIDENT

The accident left me wondering why I was placed on this Earth. I then planned my career pivot to teaching high school math.

The thing is, whatever you learned in that moment of clarity is still in you, somewhere, though it no longer takes a front seat in your awareness. And it still has things to teach you.

So, when I work with clients, I always have them go back and look for moments of clarity in their lives. I have them chronicle each one and what it taught them.

Then, because these moments might not be as dramatically clear in a career situation, I have them go back and chronicle information about every job they've ever held.

You'd be amazed at the patterns that emerge. Try this. Fill out your own job history using these criteria.

START OF JOB

1. **Description:** Briefly summarize the job and its duties. Why did you take this job?

2. **Influenced by:** Who or what influenced you to take this job? How did you find this job? A colleague? Online site? Headhunter?

3. **Feel:** What was the environment? How did it make you feel?

4. **Team or Solo:** Were you part of a team or were you on your own? What was your role? Were you the team leader or a participant? How well did the team function? Did you like being on this team?

5. **Independence:** Were you free to control how you did your job, or were the rules created for you?

6. **Manager's Style:** How did your manager or supervisor lead? What was their style?

26

7. **Work Pace/Schedule:** Did you have control of your schedule? How varied were your activities during the course of a day? How much physical activity did this job require?

8. **Rewards:** Did you feel valued? If so, what actions by your employer demonstrated to you that your contribution was valued?

9. **Best thing about this job.**

10. **Worst thing about this job.**

11. **What you learned about what you need.**

12. **What you learned about what you do *not* need.**

END OF JOB

1. **Reason you left this job.**

2. **Who or what influenced you to leave?**

3. **Did you have another job to go to when you left?**

If you do this for every position or job you have ever had and put your answers in order, you will see a pattern. Most of us have made the same mistakes in our careers more than once. I call this Career Insanity: doing the same thing over and over but expecting a different outcome each time.

In Sam's case, he realized that his spouse may not be as tickled about selling everything and becoming a vagabond as he is. They had a big house in Connecticut and upper middle-class lifestyle. He decided to look for another job and give them a couple of years to figure out what kind of a life they want going forward.

Moments of clarity are moments when your perception shifts. You're likely to have one after reflecting back on your life and your career. You're likely to see patterns and missed opportunities that have brought you to where you are now.

Take this as a moment of clarity. What do you want to do from today on?

ACTION STEPS

friday morning b4 layoff convo

✓ Retrace the moments when you suddenly saw life differently. These could be because of a problem, like an illness or layoff, or something good, like marriage or the birth of a child.

✓ Write down what you learned in those moments, whether you followed the lessons they taught or ignored them, and what the results were.

✓ Retrace your job history. What did you learn about yourself and your needs from each of the jobs you've held? Use the job history form found in the Repurpose Your Career Resource Center.

For additional resources, check out the Repurpose Your Career Resource Center at CareerPivot.com/RYC-Resources.

TO GET WHAT YOU NEED, YOU MUST KNOW WHAT YOU NEED

To paraphrase Lewis Carroll, "If you don't know where you're going, any road will get you there." But if you're tired of wandering around, never arriving at your goal, you need to figure out where you really want to be.

What do you actually need and want out of life and what role does your job play in that? This is a much bigger question than most people think. It's not just about pay, perks, or a nice boss. Many of us have a host of underlying needs we never recognize. In fact, people are often really surprised by what assessments reveal about their deepest needs. Then, after a moment of reflection, the light goes on: "Oh, THAT's what that is! I never had a name for it before."

One woman I worked with, who thought she was immune to status, learned she REALLY valued aligning herself with key decision-makers and knowing who was in charge of every project. When that didn't work out, she felt frustrated, but she couldn't say why.

30

Many people really need to be in charge of their own schedules and organizational systems. If they can't, they're constantly frustrated.

Not getting what you need isn't always as obvious as having an abusive boss or unsanitary working conditions, but it can create low-grade anxiety and frustration all day, every day, that builds up.

You can transform your work life by seeking what you really need from the job—whether that's within your current occupation or in a new one. But you have to figure out what that is and learn how to ask for it.

REWARDS

Often, we change jobs because we don't feel valued. We want and need some kind of reward for doing good work:

- The right mission.

- Bonus or financial reward.

- Public recognition or an award.

- Pat on the back and thanks from management.

- Pat on the back and thanks from your peers.

- Pat on the back and thanks from your customer.

For me, the best reward is a pat on the back from my customer. After my epiphany with my bicycle accident, I became a high school math teacher. There, my customers were my students.

In case you haven't heard, students outside of Afterschool Specials and Hallmark ads rarely thank their teachers. But in my second year, my previous year's students did come back and thank me for taking extra time with them, communicating in a way that was relevant to them, and redefining rules to help them succeed.

That first year, working long days without ever getting the reward that met my needs was torture. I didn't understand my needs at the time, so I couldn't put a finger on what was making life so stressful. In an urban school, on a new job, there are plenty of places to assign stress. Had I known what was really getting to me, I could have worked on coping mechanisms that would have helped a lot.

I have a client who got more and more depressed because his boss never told him he was doing a good job. Because he's the kind of person who tells people, verbally, when they're doing well, he has an expectation that if he's doing well someone will tell him. If they don't, he fears it means he's screwing up, in danger of getting fired, or at the very least not thought of highly. Regardless of other signs he was excelling, the fact that his boss didn't say anything constantly tugged at him. I told him to tell his boss, which he was reluctant to do. Finally, though, he walked into his boss's office and said, "I was just wondering ... you never really say much about my performance ... how am I doing?"

"Great!" his boss replied enthusiastically. "We're really pleased with your work."

"Oh," my client replied. "Would you mind telling me from time to time? It's very helpful."

His boss responded "Sure!" And then he looked at my client earnestly and said, "Thank you for telling me."

Most managers want to know how to manage better, and they can't really figure out all their different employees' feedback styles.

Some people never care about verbal feedback, but they do expect raises and bonuses. Others are most concerned about the reward of being recognized as a valuable team member. These people tend not to push for higher financial compensation, which can lead to pay inequity.

I had a client whose boss never gave raises. But he gave bonuses. That was the boss's preferred method of handling money. It was not my client's. He was looking for the security of an increased paycheck.

Some people are best rewarded by time off or more time for themselves. Others crave more challenging projects or the chance to learn new skills.

For those in the nonprofit world or in the military, the most important reward is often working on a mission that resonates with them.

What kind of reward system have you been accustomed to and how did it suit you? Was there a reward you wish you'd received more of?

FREEDOM

Freedom is ... the ability to take a two-hour client lunch without explaining it to anybody, go to a doctor's appointment without a big hassle, take Friday afternoon off, and make it up Saturday morning. Or it can be the freedom to use your imagination in creating products and solutions. Or the freedom to wear yoga pants on the job, work from home, or to speak your mind without multi-layered corporate censure. Really, freedom can be defined many ways. Most of those definitions fall roughly into three areas:

- Freedom from micromanagement, supervisors constantly telling you how to do your job.

- Freedom to be creative and individualistic in your approach.

- Freedom to create the level of structure and rules in your role.

I work with a lot of very experienced professionals who need all three kinds of freedom. They want to do the job and for everyone else to get out of the way. As long as their results meet or exceed expectations, they don't want to answer to anyone.

Freedom is increasingly important to employees. Several new approaches to management, with flatter hierarchies, make it possible for employees at all levels to essentially design their own jobs as long as the work gets done.

If you could create your own job description in terms of freedom, what would it include?

RESPECT AND EMOTIONAL SUPPORT

When we go to work, we expect our peers to treat us in a way that makes us feel that we belong.

Some of us prefer a culture where others talk to us very directly, with minimal emotion: "Just give me the facts." That communicates respect for our position.

Other people hate that way of communicating. They want their feelings and perceptions to be included in the conversation. Most people fall somewhere in between. How can you select a job and environment where you will get the respect and emotional support you want and need?

You can use strategic networking, which we'll talk about in a later chapter, to explore different environments, to assess how people communicate in those environments, and to determine what level of emotional support they offer. You could ask someone who works at a company you're interested in about their supervisor's communication style. Even if the person has a problem with the supervisor, and is being careful about expressing it, you can usually read between the lines. Look for keywords. If people talk about a "direct, no-nonsense, efficient and professional" style, you can figure that's what they seek in a candidate. If the sound of that relaxes you, you might be a good fit. If, on the other hand, someone talks about a "warm, supportive, relational" workplace, you can bet that emotions are welcome there.

VARIETY

Do you like to multitask at work? One of the key happiness factors at work is how much variety you are afforded. I have many clients who NEED lots of variety and love to multitask. I, on the other hand, like to work steadily on one project with very few interruptions.

My client, Sally was a communication expert who needed lots of variety. When she got a job at a chamber of commerce that had fewer than 50 employees, she was in heaven. They had her creating and executing email marketing campaigns, writing press releases, doing social media—she might have five kinds of tasks in a day. It was wonderful. Then they started hiring more people. Her job shrank and became much more specialized. Eventually her job consisted of doing the same few tasks over and over, and she was bored. She had learned some key things about herself in the chamber of commerce job: she loves variety and she's easily distracted. She works best by herself, in her own office, on a multitude of tasks.

Sally started looking for a new job that fit that description. But then an unexpected opportunity caught her eye. A large company wanted her to manage a staff of 12 people. It would not have much variety. She'd be working in an open office with others, instead of in her own private office.

She'd never considered a job like that and she was flattered that they trusted her to manage 12 people. She was thinking about taking the job, even though it had none of the things she was looking for.

"Do you want to manage 12 people?" I asked her.

Her face fell. No, she didn't. Not really. The idea was attractive, but she knew she much preferred working on her own.

"Could you handle an open office?" I pressed. Another "no."

Taking a job because of the idea of it is like committing to a serious relationship with an interesting stranger. By the time you figure out you actually hate the reality, you're in for a painful process to get out of it. Sally needed to focus her search on smaller companies that needed fewer people who could wear a lot more hats.

Another client of mine, Rick, is a structured anarchist. You would never know it to look at him. Every time I've seen him, every hair is in place; his clothes are impeccable. He is the former CFO of some major nonprofits, with an MBA in finance, and comes across as the most orderly person you could ever meet. His Birkman profile (a behavior and personality assessment I have all my clients do) showed what I already suspected: Structure is really important to him.

But Rick doesn't particularly care for walking into a situation that's already orderly. He prefers to impose his own order on things. He loves to walk into a situation that's in chaos and clean it up. Once it's cleaned up and running smoothly, he's bored.

He'd been hired to come in and straighten out messes before, but it never dawned on any of his previous employers that once one problem was solved, it would behoove them — and make Rick extremely happy — to find him a new mess. So, he would get a new job, clean up the chaos, and then get frustrated. Eventually he would quit and embark on another job search. When we looked at his previous jobs — why he took each one, why he left—a pattern began to emerge.

Rick, it turned out, is a "firefighter," someone who loves to stop a mundane course of work in order to "put out a fire." The financial world isn't accustomed to hiring firefighters, because if your financial situation is a mess, investors, stockholders and customers get alarmed. But in the engineering world, where I'm from, fighting fires is normal: a fellow former IBM employee, for example, got a job as director of software for another company. They'd put her on a problem project, she'd fix it and then they'd move her to the next problem. She loved her job.

Rick's employer was not accustomed to this approach, however. His company was having issues with their channel partners. His boss was planning to do a survey to identify the issues. Rick stepped in and said, "Wait. First, let me interview the top 10 channel partners. From that interview, I'll create a survey to identify the top 25 issues and actions we can take to resolve them."

s process revealed specific problems, and
ped him form a list of actions the company
ild take — from training employees to
iproving communication — to significantly boost
the value of channel partner relationships. The
information about what Rick had done went all the
way up to the CEO, who said: "You're the only
person who could have figured this out. We've
been trying to solve these problems for 10 years!"

Then Rick knew what he wanted. He wanted to
keep solving hard problems, wherever they
cropped up in the company. It took Rick and the
company a year to figure out where he belonged.
But once they did, he couldn't have been happier.

Are you a person who wants a lot of variety? Do
you get distracted easily? Do you get bored easily?
Here are a few questions to ask yourself:

- Are you more or less productive when you
  have lots of things going on simultaneously?
  Many people instinctively say more. But are
  you sure?

- At what point does multitasking become
  stressful? Is it when you have three things
  going on at the same time? Five? Ten?

- What happens when you are interrupted
  frequently? Do you become stressed?

When I was teaching high school, my day was pretty regimented. I was doing the same thing all day. In my second year of teaching, I had five sections of Algebra II, which meant I taught the same lesson five times. This would drive some people crazy, but it fit well with my personality. My schedule was decided for me down to the minute. And that was okay, because I got to be on my feet all day.

Again, that would drive some people crazy. But I can't sit at a desk for more than 45 minutes at a time. I loved that I was on my feet and moving all day.

Think about what the your perfect culture would be, based on past positive experiences and relationships at work, on teams, or personally. These give you some good insights as to what your needs are. Then you have to learn to ask for them.

ACTION STEPS

✓ Reflect on the job or position that made you feel most rewarded. What did you receive that made you feel good?

✓ Write down what you need from a job, including such intangibles as freedom, respect, physical activity, and variety.

✓ Write down the kind of culture you prefer to work in: small or large company, institutional or entrepreneurial, etc.

✓ Download the Career Reflection worksheet from the Repurpose Your Career Resource Center.

For additional resources, check out the Repurpose Your Career Resource Center at CareerPivot.com/RYC-Resources.

WHAT IS YOUR PERSONAL
OPERATING SYSTEM?

Most of my clients have a whole system of needs, stressors, and behaviors they are only marginally aware of. These things are constantly humming in the background, like the operating system of a computer. We don't think about them, but they impact everything about the way we feel and function.

One person might be extremely deliberate about making decisions. They research every car on the market before buying one. They weigh every variable, constantly looking for opportunities or pitfalls others miss. It's how they've always been. Trying to make a decision faster makes them anxious. They worry about making mistakes that could have dire consequences.

At work, they get frustrated with their boss, who seems to expect them to do hours of research to prepare for questions the boss might throw at them at meetings. From the employee's vantage point, the boss wants input and decisions on issues they couldn't possibly have had time to weigh carefully.

43

In truth, the boss doesn't expect hours of research. The boss makes decisions quickly on the facts at hand and expects employees to do the same. Such a thing would never dawn on this employee. It's too crazy, capricious, stressful.

This employee doesn't realize they need a job where their thoroughness would be an asset. They just think they need to get away from this boss.

That's where assessments come in so handy.

FIRST STEP TO CAREER BLISS: KNOW THYSELF

Many of us go after jobs thinking things like this: "I want to get away from my boss. I want more money. I want to work for a bigger organization, or a smaller one." We think we uncovered the problem with our last job or career, so we set out to solve the problem we identified.

But frequently, all we've really done is isolate a symptom, not the problem itself.

To find a career that will satisfy you in the long run, you need to understand many things about yourself: what you need, what stresses you, and what makes you happy. Assessments reveal truths about us that we might not even realize affect our careers. They can be a first step to understanding yourself, which is the first step to pursuing your own happiness and satisfaction.

I have done a bunch of assessments: MBTI (Myers-Briggs), DiSC, Kolbe, StrengthsFinder 2.0, and Birkman. For me, the most valuable for gaining insight into my own needs was the Birkman.

When I took it, several years ago, I learned that I need plenty of alone time. I had no idea. I knew that, as a younger man, I'd been alone more than I liked. And I knew that I didn't enjoy my first job at IBM alone in a cubicle. I can also tell you I am quite social. I love to work a crowd and go to many gatherings every week. (In Austin, where I live part of the time, you could attend about 1,000 a week if you had the time and stamina). What I didn't realize until I took the Birkman was that it's not an either/or. I didn't like being alone all the time. Nor could I just leap into constant social activity. I need a good balance of both.

That's a piece of information that could save me from many dissatisfying job changes. Without it, I could think: "I HATE being alone in my cubicle all day. I need a job where I'm working with people!" Then I go after a job to solve my isolation problem and wind up in meetings, client calls, or networking events from morning till night, exhausted and longing for my monastic cubicle.

That's the kind of thing the Birkman reveals. The Birkman is 298 fairly repetitious questions that ask what you do, think, and believe, and what you think "most people" do, think, and believe.

For example, "Do you think it's more important to be honest than to avoid hurting people's feelings? Do you think others feel honesty is more important that protecting people's feelings?"

It's a strange test that, after you've been asked the same question about four different ways, can make you think, "Who knows? Who cares? Why are you asking this again?"

But then you sit down with a Birkman advisor who explains what your answers say about you. The information is both surprising and familiar. It's like having a psychic tell you things that maybe you didn't want to know, but, to be honest, you already sort of knew them, deep down.

I had a client who landed in the wrong career because of things he didn't know about himself. In high school, he scored really high on the math portion of his PSAT. "Get thee to an engineering school," a counselor told him. So, he did.

Here's what the counselor wasn't aware of: In addition to being good at math, this guy is also a very empathetic, emotional person. Most engineers are very low on the empathy scale. Over the years, he learned to act like his colleagues, but

46

he was miserable. The Birkman confirmed that empathy wasn't a weakness in his work social skills; it was a strength he had to hide because of the environments he'd chosen. Now he could look for a career where both his engineering skills and his empathy would prove valuable.

ADJUSTING FOR YOUR POS

There was a great article in *Fortune* magazine on the value of the Birkman called "Are You a Good Fit for Your Job?"

Senior Editor Jennifer Reingold learned — among other things — that while she prefers taking the direct approach with others, she's not too thrilled when she's on the receiving end.

As it turns out, that's true for a lot of salespeople, too. Salespeople have to sit back and listen at first until they gain the confidence of their prospect; then lean in and start to push. This may have nothing to do with their personalities. Either the listening or the pushing might be totally opposed to how they are naturally. They have to learn to do it because that's the dynamic of sales. But frequently they don't like being a recipient of the very same treatment.

A lot of us learn to behave in ways that aren't natural for us for the sake of our jobs. Sometimes that makes us miserable. Other times we just need to learn some important coping skills.

For example, when I do speaking engagements, I usually network a lot before and after my talk. When I stand up in front of all those people and say: "I am an introvert," it always gets a laugh.

But I *am* an introvert.

I can schmooze and socialize with the best of them, but I had to learn how to do it and, ultimately, it exhausts me. I enjoy being around people. But that's not where I get my energy. I get my energy from time alone. And that is the definition of an introvert.

Our society is biased toward extroverts. Extroverts make more money. They're taken more seriously as leaders. They're perceived as more competent, even though, as Susan Cain pointed out in her book *Quiet: The Power of Introverts in a World That Can't Stop Talking,* some of the greatest CEOs like Steve Jobs and Bill Gates have been introverts.

Cain tells a story of an exercise at Harvard Business School in which a class formed two teams. The professor told the teams to pretend they were on a plane that had crashed in the Alaskan wilderness. They had to decide what to take with them from the wreckage to survive. One team member actually grew up in Alaska and had spent time in the wilderness. He knew exactly what to take. But he was an introvert, and no one asked him. When the teams reported back, the professor learned that one team member was a native Alaskan but that he had not weighed in on what to bring. When he asked why, the team leader said: "He never spoke up."

Cain's point was that the world is missing out by not making an effort to engage with introverts. But there's another point here, too: If you're an introvert, you need to find a way to cope so that you don't become the one who is missing out. Cain, herself an introvert who pretended to be an extrovert, suggests that introverts, if they're going to be around people, need little restorative niches during the day to do something they enjoy.

I had a client who loved to knit. I recommended that she take a few moments between some of her back-to-back meetings to knit. Another client had to present six times at a conference. We decided he should take breaks in between, go back to his room and read a book. For another client, the break was to take pictures—just that little act of observing gave her needed distance from the crowd.

I had one client who was a top-level sales rep married to another top-level sales rep. They both acted like extroverts, but she was a closet introvert. At a conference when everybody else was gearing up to go out to dinner, he was ready to join them, but she was done. She couldn't handle one more social interaction. She would head back to the hotel room and order room service. He would tell everyone she wasn't feeling well — because, in their world, that's better than being an introvert.

In July of 2010, I went on a grueling trip to Australia to teach a four-day sales class. At the end of each day, some of the Aussie salespeople wanted to take me out for drinks. It would have been fun, but I knew I had to say no. I had a quiet dinner with a few close friends and went back to my room to watch the Tour de France. Like my sales-rep client, I knew this was what I had to do to properly take care of myself.

There are actually a lot of us introverts out there in extrovert clothing. We can act extroverted a lot more easily, and become much more resilient, when it comes to social situations, if we make an adjustment and give ourselves breaks.

GETTING THE RIGHT PROGRAM
FOR YOUR POS

Figuring out what makes your personal operating system run well is a giant factor in being happy in your career.

Many of the women I work with (and, in fact, many women I talk to) are "stealth competitors." They were raised to believe that if they worked hard, people would recognize their contributions and reward them. Their peers would characterize these women as very "sweet." They are affable, get along well with others, never hog the limelight. They just seem content to do their jobs. If asked, that's how they might describe themselves.

But the Birkman often shows that these women are frustrated and angry. They don't understand why they're not getting recognition, praise and raises. The signals they're sending out—what the Birkman calls their "effective behavior"— communicate that they are perfectly fine without the kinds of rewards other people receive. They may have even been hired because they seemed like they would ask very little. And that's what they get. When they see those results, my clients always look shocked. "That's true!" they exclaim.

These women often don't realize that they are holding their bosses or clients accountable to give recognition and rewards that they've never asked for, or even seemed to need. This could really hurt their work relationships if they don't understand and adjust for it. But the Birkman spells all of that out. A Birkman advisor would explain that these women need to ask for what they want. That's not always easy, as we'll talk about later. But it's crucial for their happiness.

A lot of men and women succeed in their fields because they are highly organized. They can easily prioritize tasks and focus their attention and energy where it will be most effective in that moment. These people aren't at all intimidated by having a lot to do, as long as they get to decide how to do it. But give a person like that a boss who is trying to "help" by writing out a detailed list of tasks and you will have one stressed-out employee. The boss has just hobbled his best racehorse. The Birkman often shows these highly organized people that they must insist on a position where the culture or the boss will allow them to say: "Point me toward the goal and get out of my way." Then, watch 'em go!

If, on the other hand, you're someone who feels uncomfortable with a lot of autonomy, if you prefer that your boss spell out their expectations very clearly, so you don't have to make a lot of decisions that might lead to mistakes, the boss with the detailed list would be ideal.

Some people function beautifully with a lot of distractions. They might like listening to music while they work, welcome co-workers dropping by with questions, and switch easily from one quick task to the next.

Other people, me included, need stretches of uninterrupted work time to accomplish our best results. Being interrupted all the time shatters our thoughts and leaves us almost too frustrated to get anything done. Some people may not even realize that that's something they need to consider when looking at a job or career change. Is this a position where you could focus intensely for several hours or are you likely to be interrupted by customers or colleagues?

Spend time considering how you work best. It can make all the difference in the world in terms of job satisfaction and performance.

There are a number of remarkable things my clients have discovered from the Birkman. One woman found she was much happier in her job when she had a desk by the window and could bring plants to her work area.

Another client discovered that it really made her mad when someone with less expertise stepped in on decisions about her part of a project. After taking her assessment and learning the results, she knew she would still have to deal with that from team members or clients, but she was prepared to devise ways to handle it without getting upset.

STILL LEARNING FROM THE BIRKMAN

It took me months to internalize the information I learned about myself in the Birkman report, with the help of my advisor. I still go back and review my report, and I STILL am learning about myself.

One thing I've learned over time is that I have an unusual competency with reading the Birkman. Many of the people who do the sort of thing I do have backgrounds in social work, psychology, or counseling. They rely more on their intuition and people skills. But I'm a recovering engineer and I read patterns. At this point, I can meet with someone and learn a lot about them from just a few pieces of information. If they are a closet creative—someone who might have submerged their creative instincts for the sake of a paycheck-- the following things are probably true: They want a lot of respect, are an introvert, are fairly emotional, are a stealth competitor, don't like order, don't want a boss, want lots of variety, and want the freedom to do it their way. Of course, people surprise me, and I walk in with an open mind, but the patterns generally hold.

The Birkman has also given me other tools to help people understand themselves. I worked with a client who used to work for a hedge fund but loved redecorating rooms. She thought she was a creative thinker. I could tell she wasn't. She was a linear, conceptual thinker. So, I gave her a task that I give many clients: "Go find three problems you solved at work, and three in your personal life. How did you solve them? What was your thought process?"

She talked about how she approached redecorating a room: "First, I look at the colors, and then I look at the shapes in the room, and then I look at the arrangement, and then..."

I looked at her and said, "So you have a process that you follow."

She said, "I do not!"

"You just described a detailed process that you follow."

She looked at me in surprise.

"Oh, you are right."

I had another client who is now a UX designer. She thought of herself as a process-oriented thinker. I asked her how she found her apartment.

She looked at prices and then locations. She came up with a list of apartment buildings and looked at them one by one. But when she walked into her current place, she "just knew it was right."

She was, in fact, highly intuitive. She had some problem-solving processes that were linear, but she also used her intuition a lot more than she knew.

When you understand these things about yourself, it helps you make much better decisions that are likely to have much better outcomes. It's fun, too!

What could a Birkman or similar assessment tell you that would set you on not just a new path or a different path, but on the *right* path?

ACTION STEPS

✓ Take a career assessment test, such as the Birkman, to uncover rules and motivators you didn't even know you had: your personal operating system.

✓ Listen to a feedback session with a real individual. You will find links to podcast episodes where you can listen to multiple individuals' Birkman feedback sessions including their reports in the Repurpose Your Career Resource Center.

✓ Contact me at careerpivot.com/contact-me to schedule an assessment.

For additional resources, check out the Repurpose Your Career Resource Center at CareerPivot.com/RYC-Resources.

CAREER MISTAKES: FAILURE IS A GREAT OPTION

There's a gripping moment in the movie *Apollo 13* where Flight Director Gene Kranz (played by Ed Harris) is telling his Houston team that they have to figure out a way to bring the crew back.

"Failure is not an option!" he barks.

That's probably true if you're Mission Control for a bunch of people floating in a dead spaceship. In fact, Kranz named his autobiography *Failure Is Not an Option: Mission Control from Mercury to Apollo 13 and Beyond*. That mentality is fortifying and inspiring, like Cortez burning the ships. My generation grew up with that, "Never surrender. Never accept failure," credo. But the truth is, these days, it's mostly bullshit.

If you're like most people, failure is sometimes not only an option, but it's inevitable. And to take it one step further, it's essential. You don't learn unless you fail. And unless you're willing to fail, you aren't likely to venture anything very impressive. Some of my biggest leaps forward began with tripping. I can pinpoint the moments of my biggest career failures. And because I went back and analyzed them, like the good recovering engineer that I am, I can see how each one propelled me forward. Here they are:

MISTAKE ONE: I WAS SEDUCED BY A FORMER MANAGER

To be clear, I'm a happily married man. But in the late 1990s, when I was working for IBM in a briefing center, I was bored. My job was to give the inside scoop on various products to IBM's leading customers. For me, it was an easy job. The presentations were deeply technical, but I understood them and crafted the information into six or seven presentations that I could have given in my sleep.

The great part of the job was that, as an ambassador for our top clients, I was highly visible to upper management. For that reason, they often asked me to present at leading conferences. I got tons of swag: jackets, shirts, hats, bags...

But after seven years of doing this job, I was ready for a new challenge.

My manager (who was great) had left the previous year to work for IBM Global Services, the IBM consulting arm. She knew I was bored and worked on me to join her group. She painted a very rosy picture, so, after about six months, I made the leap. It was one of the biggest mistakes of my career.

I had allowed myself to be seduced, as did several other people she knew in the organization who had deep consulting experience. I don't think she intended anything negative for me. But I should have done my homework rather than just accepting her description of the job. I realized that almost as soon as I took it.

The job required me to sit for long hours developing technical proposals, a task for which I did not have the attention span. I also really suck at writing technical proposals, possibly because I don't like sitting around developing them. My first set of proposals was lambasted, not because of the technical stuff, but because of the writing.

I also couldn't pick my projects. I was put on a team developing a point-of-sale solution for a national short-term loan company (pawnshop). The more I learned about the business, the more I wanted out of there. Loaning money to the poor at 20 percent a month (not 20 percent a year, like credit card providers) made me ill.

Finally, I had really enjoyed my previous team at the briefing center, but my new team comprised mostly unhappy single people, unhappy divorced people, and unhappy married people. Most of them had traveled too much in their careers and had poor personal relationships. Not fun. I missed my old team.

Then one day, about six months in, my young project manager tried to humiliate me in front of the team for my poor writing skills. So, I quit. I quit the project and I quit being a consultant.

It took me two months to find another position within the marketing division of IBM, but even as I took the job, I knew this was a holding place. Less than a year later, I left IBM after 22 years to go to work for a successful semiconductor startup.

MISTAKE TWO: TAKING MY DREAM JOB

Big mistake number two was going full bore after what I believed to be my dream job. You know dream jobs: working in the embassy in Paris, owning a B&B, being a recruiter for the NFL. They look perfect, like career Valhalla, except most of us choose a dream job without ever investigating what it actually entails. We suffer from MSU (Making Stuff Up) Disorder, which we'll talk about in a later chapter. My dream job was more of the *To Sir, With Love, Stand and Deliver, Freedom Writers* variety. I went to teach high school math in an inner-city school.

I had been developing curriculum and teaching engineers on-and-off for 20-plus years in about 35 different countries. Heck, if I could train engineers in the People's Republic of China, I was sure I could teach Algebra I and II to teenagers. And I could. But that's not all you have to know about the job you're going into.

First of all, no one told me that the average math teacher in Texas leaves the profession in fewer than five years. When I asked teachers about their experiences, they sugarcoated their answers. They didn't tell me that being an experienced 40-something can be a bad thing in a school system, where administrators prefer to deal with compliant, new grads. They didn't warn me that the hiring process was obscure and convoluted, and when I went through the alternative certification process at my local community college, my gut was telling me that I was not going to be prepared.

Most of all, I was not prepared for the trauma of working with a bunch of kids whose problems in life were far beyond what I could get my head around or do anything about. I thought that since I was an expert in multiple cultures, a veteran instructor, and a tough guy, I could handle it. The culture of poverty introduced me to things beyond what I could handle.

I was good at what I did. I had a tremendous success rate and I touched many lives. That's the whole reason I went into the job in the first place. If that had been enough, I'd still be there. But the whole experience tore me up emotionally and physically. What made it worse was that the mentors who got me through the first year were all gone the next fall. I thought I could handle it without them. I was wrong. In hindsight, I should have quit at the end of my first year.

But I am a Baby Boomer. When we undertake to do a thing, we have to see it through or be a "quitter." I tried to follow the immortal words of Winston Churchill: "Never, never, never give up." You stick it out until you have no choice but to leave. New information: When it comes to picking a job, you should give up before then.

Former colleagues often told me they planned to follow in my footsteps and become teachers when they retired. Most dream jobs are mistakes waiting to happen.

MISTAKE THREE: I CAN MAKE THIS WORK

The next of my mistakes was to take a job that was not optimal, telling myself I could make it work. I had gone into teaching to do something meaningful. When I left, I still wanted to do something meaningful. So, I looked for a job with a nonprofit. Since I had spent a considerable amount of my previous 15 years in sales support, I thought I'd be great at a fundraising position. By the way, there are way too many nonprofits in

Austin, and most have either no salaried positions, or very few.

I pursued jobs at organizations with missions aligned with my own values. But I got nowhere. I broadened my search to include nonprofits that were "close enough."

Soon, I was hired by the local Jewish community center to build a corporate giving program. It is a worthy organization, but I'd chosen it because it was a nonprofit with a job, not because it was doing something I was already excited about. Its mission, while good, isn't really aligned with what's important to me. And frankly, being a non-Jew as the face for a Jewish organization was … interesting! Austin has very few Jewish-owned businesses, which made it even more difficult. Plus, I saw telltale signs of the impending great recession. All of the banks I approached were very friendly, but kindly showed me the door. I had a position that would eventually be eliminated. Finally, I was rapidly figuring out that I could not tolerate the dysfunctional behavior of nonprofits. I was used to getting things done, but that is not how things typically work in nonprofits.

After six months, I decided I would leave right after the big fall gala. I would take vacation and then turn in my resignation. I lasted a year, but I made the decision pretty early on that this was not for me. Despite what I told myself, I could not make it work.

FAILURE'S UPSIDE

Actually, I am happy I took all three jobs. I learned a tremendous amount about consulting, public education and nonprofits. I learned a lot about myself:

- My team is really important.

- I do not have unlimited energy to muscle through difficult situations.

- The mission is really important to me.

Very few of us just hop from one career into the perfect one without some experimentation.

My client Mike, for example, was a B2B sales guy. A lot of those types of jobs have disappeared because procurement experts do their own online research rather than having a salesperson explain why their option is better. Mike started thinking about some other careers. He had an associate degree in aviation and decided to go back and get his bachelor's.

"If it has wings, wheels or keels," he said, "it's for me." Mike read a lot of articles about a guy who got a job on the British tube system and how he had prepared himself. Then he learned that the

Houston METRORail system was opening up its Red Line and needed train drivers. He got the job, and he loved it. But his wife still lived in Austin and he lived in Houston. So, after a year, he started looking for something else.

Now he's preparing to become a drone pilot who teaches people how to fly drones. They're used in so many things: construction, conservation, and agriculture, just to name a few. The world is wide open for Mike, and he's having a lot of fun designing his pivot.

Failing, experimenting, and reinventing can be an adventure. But you need your infrastructure in place, which I lacked. I came up with a plan, based on my mistakes, that can help anyone who is getting ready to make a Career Pivot.

RULES OF REINVENTION

Have a Plan B: Be prepared to pull the plug on the reinvention project. Have a clear timeline and metrics to determine your success. For example, you might have five goals you're working on in terms of finances, skills learned, or happiness. Give yourself short windows to achieve these and evaluate realistically. If you're not hitting them, it's time to rethink your plan.

Don't wait to develop your Plan B in the middle of taking a new job; have it in place from day one.

Make sure the work you're doing is something that you could use to pivot into something else. The big fear is moving away from your skill set and falling behind without building anything you can use in your next job if this one doesn't work out. Keep your network fresh, even as you're working in a new job or industry.

With the bad consulting job, I knew that I could find a position in the division I left within IBM. It took two months, and the consulting group did not push me to find anything quickly. That was a solid Plan B. With the teaching job, there was no Plan B.

I had left my tech job two years before, which meant that I was already out of date. With my nonprofit, I decided to leave several months before I actually did, and knew I wanted to take a few months to rest. In the fall, I was approached with three technology opportunities. Quickly, I had multiple Plan Bs! I took a long vacation and was hired in December 2007 by a tech startup to develop a training and certification program.

Think through your Plan B carefully. I have had several clients who took "survival" jobs while they figured out what they wanted to do. But some of these survival jobs were with companies that had constantly changing schedules. One of my clients, Dave, did this. He took a job at a home supply discount store, thinking it would be fun to work there for a while. But because he never knew when he would be working from week to week, he could never schedule meetings with me, meetings with other people in his network, or job interviews. The job turned out to be a trap.

If this sort of thing happens, you need a plan to escape.

Learn from your mistakes: The way you turn a mistake into something good is by learning from the experience. You always have to take stock of choices and actions from your past and what you can take away that will make tomorrow's choices and actions better. I learned a ton from my mistakes.

From the bad consulting job, I learned how important a team was to me, what kinds of work I don't like, and that you have to do your homework before you take a job. I actually relearned all those lessons in teaching. But I also realized it stimulated my entrepreneurial juices to be in this old battleship called public education. I mentored my principal as we went through a high school redesign. It was clear to me that I would eventually work for myself to fix real-world problems. I also learned that I did not have the emotional stamina to work with teenagers who had problems most of us cannot even imagine.

At the nonprofit, I learned that I really need to understand how organizational rules apply to a job before I take it. I assumed that I could get groups within the organization to work with me, to do things differently, to think a little differently — boy, was I wrong! Working inside of a nonprofit was not for me.

Failure is an option, but fail fast: In the tech world the rallying cry is, "fail fast, fail often." If you have that mentality, it means you're someone who is going to take some risks and try for big things. This mentality is very hard for someone who grew up in the 1960s and 1970s to adopt. We were taught to be risk averse.

I had a discussion with a franchising consultant a couple of years ago. He told me about the people he met in 2002-2004 who had been laid off after the dot-com bubble burst. Many of them had a lot of money in retirement accounts and asked him about starting franchises. His advice was to invest no more than 10 percent of their net worth in a franchise. Even though that was a conservative number, and many of them could afford to take the risk, they chose not to pursue it because they were terrified of failing. They were still too risk-averse to take the chance.

But the world has changed. If you were unemployed in the 1960s and did not quickly secure a new job, there was something wrong with you. Today, a huge percentage of the population has been touched by unemployment. Being unemployed is no longer a red flag on your record.

And a lot of people would rather start their own businesses than get another job where someone else has their hand on the lever of their success and failure. Before the early 2000s, the upfront investment to start a business was huge. Most people would need to take out a significant loan. If you failed, the financial and personal consequences would be huge. That is why most of us became employees.

That's no longer the case. If you have a laptop, an internet connection, and some hustle, you can start a business right now, no money down. In the last five years I have:

- Published four books with no publisher, selling four thousand copies.

- Created a website and blog that garner over 25,000 visitors a month without a major capital investment.

- Created a highly recognizable brand — Career Pivot.

All of this was done with a lot of sweat equity but a very small financial investment.

I belong to several technology meetups where new companies form almost overnight. Co-founders meet, hatch a plan for an app, sign up for Amazon Web Services, rent space at a co-working facility, and develop the product. Total investment? Less than $10,000. A decade ago, the initial investment was probably closer to $1 million or more.

And if you fail, it's not a catastrophe. But you should fail fast. In two of the three situations, I failed within six months. This greatly eased my recovery. When I forced myself to stick it out, the recovery was much more painful. You also get farther away from your skills and network.

I've talked to so many people who hung on to their reinvention until they could no longer make it. They have yet to recover. They stuck to it so long that their connections with their previous careers were lost. As the adage goes: "Don't cling to a mistake just because it took you so long to make it."

If you're not failing, you're not growing. But you have to be doing both. Have a plan, have a way to gauge whether it's working and jump ship when it isn't. Unlike with the Apollo mission, if you've planned it right, another ship will come along soon enough.

ACTION STEPS

✓ Reflect on a time when you had a career failure.

✓ Write down how you recovered.

✓ Reflect on what you could have done differently.

✓ Look at whether you have ever taken risks, and, if not, do you have regrets about that?

For additional resources, check out the Repurpose Your Career Resource Center at CareerPivot.com/RYC-Resources.

DO YOU SUFFER FROM MSU DISORDER?

My client Bill writes for a major financial company. When we were talking about his career change, he said wistfully: "My dream job is to write for *The Economist*."

"Oh?" I responded. "How do you know? Do you know someone who works there?" He didn't.

Did he know whether it was considered a great place to work? What kind of hours did the company expect from employees? Was there the opportunity to advance? What about the culture? Did he know about turnover there, or the reputation of the management or executive team?

He didn't know any of that.

"So," I said, "how the heck do you know what it is like to work there?"

"Well, I really don't," he responded. "They just write such great content. They cover the world, and they're so focused on important news and trends. I am just sure it would be a wonderful place to work."

He had read *The Economist* and fixated on working there as his dream job. In short, he was Making Stuff Up. ("Stuff" could be replaced by a four-letter Germanic-Old English word I use sometimes.)

Making Stuff Up (MSU) is what most of us do when we don't have actual information. When there are holes or gaps in what we know, we just fill them in with things that seem to make sense based on our hopes or fears. Often, the ideas we stuff the gaps with have absolutely nothing to do with the reality of the situation.

In her book *Conversational Intelligence: How Great Leaders Build Trust & Get Extraordinary Results*, Judith Glaser discusses how the stories we make up have a significant impact on our careers. MSU can cause you to go after a job that would make you miserable, because you didn't really research the job itself. It can keep you from pursuing a great job, because you're afraid you're unqualified. It can cause you to give up on a job you're being considered for because you assume they weren't interested or didn't like you. And it can cause other people to lose confidence in you, because you present as irrefutable fact information that has no basis. In short, it means you make decisions based on the ghosts in your head, which is generally a bad idea.

We all make stuff up sometimes, when the information's not there. It's perfectly human. But when it comes to your career, don't do it.

THE PAIN WE CAUSE OURSELVES: AWFULIZING

Bill made stuff up about a dream job. But many people make stuff up that "awfulizes" a situation. They don't know the facts, so they cook up a worst-case scenario, talk themselves into it, and proceed to freak out about the story they just made up.

Rhoda, a former CEO, applied for a job as chief operating officer of a national association. She was excited about the job and felt like the feeling was mutual. But when she didn't hear back from anyone, she looked at the association's website for clues about what might have happened. There she saw the smiling face of their senior vice president of operations. In seconds, Rhoda had a story going. They had changed their minds! They had hired someone else already! They just hadn't bothered to tell her about it. She contacted me in a panic, a whole scene playing out in her head like a movie.

"So," I asked her, "in absence of information, you decided to play detective?"

I recommended she call her contact at the company and ask about it. When she did, she learned that the senior vice president of operations was the guy she had applied to replace. He was leaving because he needed to take care of a family member. The company had decided to upgrade the position from senior vice president to COO — the role Rhoda had applied for that still wasn't filled. She never would have come up with that explanation on her own. Rhoda did get the job, by the way.

Another client, Marcos, really wanted to leave his job, but had to wait until his 55th birthday or he would lose $150,000 in pension benefits. He applied for a job, and the interview process took months.

I could tell from what he shared with me about his interactions with them that they wanted him. But it just took so long.... At one point, he simply didn't hear from anyone for several weeks. He called me in a panic: "I've lost the job!"

"What do you mean?" I asked.

"I haven't heard from them for weeks. They finally gave up. I lost the job!"

"You don't know that," I said. "All you know is that you don't know what's happening. Why don't you call the recruiter?" He did. No answer. I still encouraged him not to awfulize what was happening but acknowledge that he just didn't know. As it turned out, the recruiter's mother had gotten very ill and he'd dropped everything to take care of her.

Finally, the company told Marcos they wanted to hire him. But when he informed them he would not be able to leave his job for several weeks because of the pension they asked, "What would it take to make you whole?" They hoped they could cover the gap and get him on the job earlier. Learning that it would take $150,000, they decided they'd rather wait than pay that kind of bonus. But they decided Marcos was worth it. He did get the job.

When my client, Susan, started a new job with a major drug company, she knocked the ball out of the park. They loved her. But when the division Susan worked for, which had around 200 people, announced a 30 percent headcount reduction, she went into panic mode. Fortunately, she only had to wait one day to learn from her boss that not only would she still have her job, but she would now also lead a highly prized project. She ignored every sign that she was highly valued, even though there were a lot of signs. She just made stuff up in her head when she heard about the layoffs, which caused enormous stress.

DIRE PREDICTIONS THAT DON'T COME TRUE

My client Tania works from home. Whenever she has meetings with her boss, she brings a list of activities she's been doing, and he always criticizes them in a harsh, abusive way. It's gone on like this for years. She brings the list; he tears her down. The rest of their relationship is fine. One day I suggested she try not bringing the list. After all, according to her, he'd never asked for a list. She only brought it because she'd done so with other bosses. She thought my suggestion was crazy. If she didn't bring the list, she assured me, he'd really come after her.

"How do you know?" I asked her. She didn't. She was Making Stuff Up.

Finally, she screwed up her courage and went to the meeting without the list. She was kind of a basket case during the days before the meeting. But when she got there, without the list, he said nothing. He just took notes on her activities and didn't give her grief about it.

Tania's situation is another form of MSU I hear all the time: if/then

- If I raise the price, they'll stop hiring me.

- If I ask to work from home sometimes, they'll fire me.

- If I refuse to take on extra hours, they'll give all the good projects to someone else.

But then I ask: "How do you know? On what information are you basing this assumption?" Usually it's just the ghosts in our heads. We don't know at all.

Often our MSU thoughts seem so real, or we've rehearsed them so often, that we don't even remember that we never stopped to ask, "Where did I get this idea?"

We just get really anxious about something and it makes us feel like we have control if we can "decide" the outcome, even if it's totally made up. In fact, the only thing you can control is your response to the fact that you DON'T KNOW. Either find a way to get information or find a way to learn to live with uncertainty. There's a lot of that in life.

Learning to live with it is a good idea.

LET HISTORY GUIDE YOU

One thing that's really important with MSU is to make a mental bookmark of all the times you've been panicked about something and it turned out you were wrong. Think back to all the times you've awfulized something. Someone didn't call within a given window (that you made up) and you assumed something terrible had happened or was about to happen. You may have freaked out, chewed your nails, yelled at your family, drunk a bunch of whiskey, applied for another job you really didn't want, or eaten an entire cheesecake. Whatever. You could feel the tension rise inside you.

And the truth turned out to be nothing like the story you made up.

It's important to go back and remember those moments and how silly you felt afterward. The best thing to do in those situations is to realize that you don't know what's happening, make an effort to get answers, and try to just breathe through the moment. Admitting you don't know is a lot less crazy-making than the intense fantasies you're likely to come up with. Try to stay in the moment and accept that the truth is you don't know. And that's okay.

STOP, DROP, AND ROLL

Of course, it's hard to remember to breathe and stay in the moment when something big is on the line. That's why I suggest you remember: "Stop, drop, and roll." Do you remember when, as a kid, you were told to stop, drop, and roll should your clothes ever catch on fire? The idea was that your natural reaction to having fire on your body would be to panic and run, which would only make things worse. This easy-to-remember saying told you exactly what to do. So, before panic could set in, you'd stop, drop, and roll.

Many of us have triggers that set off panic. My client Mary has a boss who tends to be rude whenever she calls. One day, Mary was attending a conference, quite happily listening to a session, when she felt her cell phone vibrate. She looked down at the caller ID: It was her boss. This was usually a trigger for anxiety. She was going to get yelled at. Normally she would bolt out of the session and take the call, even though it was likely to be unpleasant.

This time, she remembered stop, drop, and roll. She did not know why her boss was calling. She did not know whether she'd done anything that would get her yelled at. All she knew was that she was in a session and her boss was calling. So, this time she let the call go to voicemail. She texted her boss back that she was sitting in a session and could not take her call. She then asked whether there was anything she could help her with.

Her boss replied that she, too, was coming to the conference and just wanted Mary to know. That was it. That was all.

Mary executed stop, drop, and roll flawlessly. She controlled the narrative rather than letting her boss dictate her emotional state.

MANAGING COMMUNICATION

When my client Nancy took the job she has now, the boss admitted to Nancy that she was difficult to work for. As a result, Nancy avoids the boss and only talks to her when something goes wrong. In between times, she makes up stuff in her head like:

"I am not doing a good job. My boss does not like me. They are setting me up to let me go."

Is any of this stuff true? I do not know — and neither does Nancy.

I help people find new careers, but I also can help them find more satisfaction from the jobs they already have. Nancy really likes her job, aside from the constant panic that she's not doing well. Nancy and I decided she should schedule a weekly meeting with her boss to discuss the following week's schedule. Nancy needed to talk to her boss on her own terms. She needed to manage the communication to find out what her boss really thinks. What she learned was that her boss is moody, and that most of the time her behavior toward Nancy has nothing to do with Nancy. Opening up that conversation and understanding where her boss was coming from solved a lot of Nancy's MSU.

Everybody has MSU. Even scientists and engineers who aren't supposed to ever make stuff up. It's a normal thing our brain does. The problem isn't that we make up a story. The problem is that we believe it and react to it. Instead, we need to recognize that MSU is just our brain filling in the holes and that it might not be true at all. Stop, drop, and roll. Don't get upset about the story in your head. Take a deep breath and get facts, or just admit you don't know.

One of the big issues for people in a career transition is learning to deal with the uncertainty. But you can deal with uncertainty while looking for what you really want, or while gritting your teeth and putting up with a job you really don't. I think the first one's better.

ACTION STEPS

✓ Describe a time or times when you made stuff up. Did things turn out the way you feared?

✓ Develop a "stop, drop and roll" to apply in each situation where you tend to make stuff up.

For additional resources, check out the Repurpose Your Career Resource Center at CareerPivot.com/RYC-Resources

IS IT AGEISM?

Ageism is a fact of life; and ageism in looking for work can create a lot of obstacles. In fact, the 7th U.S. Circuit Court of Public Appeals ruled in early 2019 that the Age Discrimination in Employment Act only protects current employees and does not cover external applicants. I don't know whether that ruling will stand, but it means companies can avoid being penalized for age discrimination so long as they never hire anyone over the age of 40.

According to Dictionary.com, the definition of ageism is "a tendency to regard older persons as debilitated, unworthy of attention, or unsuitable for employment." I define job search ageism as a perception — without evidence — that an older candidate is unable to do a job due to health, appearance, or skills. Notice that I said *a perception.*

We can often shape others' perceptions if we make the effort.

BEEN OFF THE LOT FOR A WHILE

I recently traded in my 2003 Honda Element DX. Everyone knows cars lose value the minute you drive them off the lot, and I'd owned this one for 13 years and put 130,000 miles on it. The dealer's estimate of the car's value included three factors:

- Mechanics

- Appearance

- Features

The vehicle's mechanics were in pretty good shape. I maintained it well. But it still had the original clutch and brakes. In checking its mechanical integrity, the dealer was basically evaluating my car's health.

The appearance was okay. It had no dents or dings, but the front seat was worn, and the windshield was cracked. Years ago, a rock flew up, chipped the glass, and created a crack across the whole windshield. It didn't affect my vision, so I left it. Still, like an older person shows their years, this was clearly not a new car.

The car lacked the latest gizmos and gadgets. In fact, it had almost no gizmos and gadgets. It was a base model with five-speed manual transmission. I'd done nothing to upgrade it, like adding a stereo or wi-fi. If you think of features as skills, my car with few features simply wasn't as valuable or sellable as cars with GPS, Bluetooth, wi-fi connectivity, and other features newer cars have.

In other words, it was a perfectly serviceable, drivable car. But just because it had some miles on it, was a little worn, and didn't have the features newer cars have, the dealer paid me less for my car than I paid in the first place. He was being ageist toward my car!

See where am I going with this?

AGEISM IN THE SECOND HALF OF LIFE

When we reach the second half of life, we may experience age discrimination or ageism. In some cases, that's because of the perception that we may be too expensive. That perception is based on our date of birth. But just like my Honda, we're evaluated for more than just our manufacture date. And it's our responsibility to do what we need to do to increase our "resale" value.

HEALTH

Just like my Honda, we're judged based on our health. Since most people don't give you a physical before they decide whether to hire you, they base their perception of your health on your appearance. How we carry ourselves, the energy we exude, our weight, the appearance of our hair, skin, and teeth all communicate something about our health. If we move slowly, have trouble getting up and down, have trouble breathing, seem tired, or generally look unwell, it may be a sign we haven't taken such good care of ourselves, and many will wonder whether we can keep up.

If we broadcast "old and worn out" during the interview, and we don't get the job, that's not ageism. On the other hand, my boss at my last corporate gig told me that the qualified trainer I was trying to hire "didn't have the energy he wanted." In this case, I knew he was using code for "too old." The candidate was approximately the same age as me. He was a bit overweight and had a bit of gray hair, but nothing extreme. This was a classic case of ageism, based on my boss's perception of the individual.

I resigned several months later.

APPEARANCE

How you dress and carry yourself is important. I have an image consultant who picks out all of my new clothes, because I lack good taste in clothes. When I hired her to evaluate colors for me, she eliminated more than half of my clothes during the wardrobe evaluation. This made my wife very happy.

When I worked at my first tech startup in 2000, I was one in a group of four people out of 100 employees who was more than 40 years old. Mine was not a customer-facing role, so I came to work in T-shirts and jeans. Because of this, I came across as a peer and not like a manager (or a parent, which is their real concern). In this instance, I managed their perceptions by how I dressed.

I have a client in her late 50s who interviewed for a position with a hedge fund manager. She didn't ask about the dress code before the interview, so she showed up dressed in a conservative business suit. The hedge fund manager, who was in her early 30s, wore torn blue jeans. Needless to say, my client didn't get the job.

SKILLS

We're hired for our skills. Just like my Honda, I didn't upgrade some of my skills. If you don't invest in learning new skills, most of the time you won't be considered for a position, even though you could easily learn these skills on the job.

Companies no longer wish to train their employees. It's the employee's responsibility to maintain their skills. This has been a major shift in the last 10 to 20 years.

NAVIGATING JOB SEARCH AGEISM

The easiest way to **combat ageism** is to focus on your health, appearance, and skills before you ever experience ageism. Follow these tips to combat ageism:

LEAD A HEALTHY LIFESTYLE

Yeah, we all know we should do this. But there are still some people who say, "Well, at my age it's normal to..." have extra weight, ignore fitness, need a lot of rest, or whatever. That's the point: you don't want to feed the narrative that your age keeps you from being your best.

DRESS APPROPRIATELY

If you need help like I do, then get help. If you don't need help but you're just not interested in updating your look, you might find that's a liability. Wearing dated clothing or hairstyles, wearing inappropriate clothing for the workplace culture, or wearing ill-fitting clothing, all contribute to a perception that you're not a fit for today's fast-paced work world.

MAINTAIN YOUR SKILLS

Stay on top of industry trends. If there's a new app, tool, collaboration software, or business model making inroads in your industry, you need to know how to use it. Younger generations believe their continuing education is their responsibility, and they'll hold you to that, too. Companies want to know you are already comfortable with the modern tools and will welcome new ones.

DON'T CALL ATTENTION TO YOUR AGE

Don't make comparisons between you and people of other generations. Don't talk about how things were done in your day. It's fine to talk about your kids; it's not fine to point out they are about the CEO's age. Behave as a professional working with other professionals and leave age out of the conversation.

UPDATE YOUR SOCIAL MEDIA AND RESUME

Resume styles change often. Make sure yours isn't sporting a 2010 look. Only include relevant skills—your ability to code in MS-DOS is not a positive. Leave off really old experience; leave dates off your resume. Instead of advertising that you've been doing something for 20 years or are a seasoned professional, point out that you learn fast and enjoy tackling new skills.

JUST PLAIN UPDATE

For me, my health was my biggest issue, and I have been focusing on that. My last tech startup left me worn out, and I looked old when I resigned! I've since been focusing on my health by eating right, exercising, seeing my chiropractor regularly, and monitoring my health. Find out what your main areas of updating need to be. Ask your peers what you need to work on to help combat job search ageism. Encourage them to be honest and help you figure out where to begin. Remember, it's not about what you think, but what *they* think! And be sure to ask those younger than you, as well as those your own age.

Discrimination sucks. It's hard to go to a job interview feeling like you're already on the defensive because of something you can't help, like your age. But if you work on improving your health, appearance, and skills you can powerfully impact others' perceptions. Plus, giving yourself a makeover might just make you feel better about yourself.

ACTION STEPS

✓ With the help of a consultant, maybe a younger person, evaluate what your appearance, health, skills, and resume communicate about who you are with regard to your age.

✓ Develop a plan to manage perception by updating your online presence as well as your physical appearance and health.

✓ Find out the new tools that are popular in your industry and get trained on them.

For additional resources, check out the Repurpose Your Career Resource Center at CareerPivot.com/RYC-Resources.

LEARN TO EMBRACE CREATIVE DESTRUCTION

In his book, *Antifragile: Things That Gain from Disorder,* Nassim Nicholas Taleb explains the problem of turkeys. A butcher, he said, feeds a turkey for 1,000 days. Every day that the turkey's life remains constant confirms the surety of his current existence: this is the way it goes; this is the way it has always gone; this is the way it will always go. All his data confirm that butchers love turkeys. The turkey can rest confident in this idea because he has 999 days of benevolent treatment to back it up. Then, a few days before Thanksgiving, everything in his worldview is upturned. This is what Taleb calls a "Black Swan" event. All the evidence proves it can't happen, until it does.

The truth is that this is the normal course of things in human existence. An old, established company closes its doors. A chronic condition suddenly manifests. A financial windfall, or unexpected romance changes your trajectory. Death comes unexpectedly. This is how life is. In the world of work, the force behind these changes is often the power of creative destruction. One thing is destroyed; another is created. The turkey's life is over; dinner is served.

If the change is something we wanted to happen, we think it's a good change. If the change is something we didn't want to happen, we think it's a bad change. Regardless of how we feel about them, though, Black Swan events are going to happen, and we need to not be taken by surprise, like the turkey.

I was listening to an episode of the *Freakonomics* podcast called "How Safe is Your Job?" The hosts were talking about pianos. In 1905, they said, 400,000 pianos were made in America. If you wanted music in your house, you learned to play the piano.

The phonograph had been created 30 years before in 1877. But phonograph sales didn't take off until 1915. A decade later the radio became popular. Today only 30,000 pianos are made each year, about eight percent of the number made in 1905. Each new iteration of musical enjoyment was a form of creative destruction. Each caused people in the previous industry to lose jobs or pivot.

In 1975, an employee of the Kodak company created a digital camera. But instead of developing it, Kodak leadership concluded it was a non-starter; they assumed people wouldn't want to look at their pictures on their TVs. So, the company continued focusing on chemical film until it became clear they had bet on the wrong horse. In 2001, Kodak had the second most popular digital camera on the market but lost $60 on every sale. A decade later, Kodak declared bankruptcy.

In these cases, creative destruction took 20, 30 or 40 years to bring down one giant and birth another. Now that pace is accelerating.

Amazon.com was founded in 1994 and initially just sold books. It was credited with the demise of several brick-and-mortar bookselling chains. Over the next 11 years, Amazon moved into retailing pretty much everything, and by 2015 it passed Walmart to be the most valuable retailer in the world by market capitalization. It took them—and their online retail competitors—only a few years to rejigger the world of shopping and knock the brick-and-mortar store off the pedestal as the cornerstone of public commerce.

In 2018, Amazon started buying surviving brick-and-mortar retailers, including Whole Foods, presumably to collect data on the people who still shop there and further strengthen their market presence. Now Amazon's opening brick-and-mortar stores around the country, including convenience stores and bookstores. It's remaking retail Amazon-style.

The iPhone was launched in 2007. At that time, I used my phone for talking to people. Today this is what I use my phone for:

- Getting the weather report from the Weather Channel app

- Managing my LinkedIn and Twitter. (I removed the Facebook app after the last presidential election.)

- Taking and viewing pictures

- Editing files in Google Drive or Dropbox

- Communicating with clients over Skype

- Checking scores on the ESPN app

- Finding my keys using the Tile app

- Listening to podcasts and audio books, as I no longer listen to the radio

- Finding the new coffee shop via Google and Apple Maps

- Entering the YMCA by swiping the bar code in the YMCA app

- Managing multiple credit cards and bank accounts

- Showing the police officer my proof of insurance via the State Farm app

- Checking airline schedules to see if a flight is on time

- Searching Google to answer the question my wife just asked me

- Watching *House Hunters International* on HGTV via the Sling TV app

- Oh, and a lot of people use their phones to listen to music

GETTING SMAC'D

Because of the technology we have now, everything is being reimagined, reconfigured, and reinvented, at a pace our parents never could have conceived of. The world is being SMAC'd:

S=SOCIAL

Today people turn to social media sites such as LinkedIn, Facebook, Twitter, Pinterest, Instagram, and Snapchat—for everything: It's the U.S. mail, the telephone, the photo album, the gossip chain, the opinion column, news, entertainment, education, and job board all rolled into one. It's also one place employers go to find you and investigate whether you're the right kind of candidate.

M=MOBILE

Roughly 60 percent of adults get their news on a mobile device, according to Pew Research Center. Mobile apps track our behavior and our preferences, as well as give us means to pay for things. People use mobile devices to shop, to bank, to date. If your career isn't mobile friendly, you will get left in the dust.

A=ANALYTICS

The amount of data collected in the last few years exceeds what was collected during the previous entire century. A lot of it is coming voluntarily from our activities via social media and mobile. How we shop, where we shop, how we pay, where we go online, and even how long it takes to get somewhere are some of the things that inform this data. Do you remember the movie *Minority Report* where Tom Cruise walks through a mall with hyper-customized ads displayed everywhere? Analytics will affect how you are hired.

C=CLOUD

The cloud is changing everything in the technology world. Most of the major technology hardware vendors are seeing portions of their business collapse because data isn't being stored on their hardware, it's being stored in the cloud. A classic example is IBM, which missed the shift and is seeing massive changes in their business. Their hardware business is collapsing.

Cloud computing is sometimes referred to as SaaS (Software as a Service). With SaaS, you don't have to buy a disc to get the software; you don't have to save data on your computer; you don't have to have a photo album, or a filing cabinet. You can keep everything in the cloud.

Articles have said for decades that the robots were going to take our jobs someday. And SMAC is robots beginning to do just that. A 2018 study by PwC predicts that nearly 40 percent of jobs in the U.S. may be vulnerable to replacement by robots in the next fifteen years.

Some people assume the jobs robots can do are severely limited.

Nope.

SURPRISING JOBS A ROBOT CAN DO

JOURNALISM

A 2017 article in *Wired* called "What News-Writing Bots Mean for the Future of Journalism" leads with this—

When Republican Steve King beat back Democratic challenger Kim Weaver in the race for Iowa's 4th congressional district seat in November, The Washington Post snapped into action, covering both the win and the wider electoral trend....

The dispatch came with the clarity and verve for which Post reporters are known, with one key difference: It was generated by Heliograf, a bot that made its debut on the Post's website last year and marked the most sophisticated use of artificial intelligence in journalism to date.

Any type of writing that is based on data can be replaced with automation and robots.

MEDICINE

Automation and robots will have an incredible impact on medical professions. If a doctor wants an EKG, you can record it on your smartphone app. All of your medical data will someday be digitized, including X-ray images, CT scans, and MRIs. Images are sent to places like India or China to be evaluated by doctors who are paid less. And automation and robots are starting to do work that doctors have always done. According to *The Economist*, a product from Enlitic can outperform doctors in reading diagnostic images.

RETAIL

Retail jobs are disappearing at an alarming rate.

- Sears closed 3,500 stores and cut about 250,000 jobs over the last 15 years before declaring bankruptcy and being forced to reorganize in 2018.

- Many specialty chains are failing, like Tailored Brands, owner of stores like Men's Wearhouse and Jos. A. Bank.
- Amazon is opening stores called Amazon Go where people can do their whole shopping trip without interacting with a single person.

As the **Fight for** 15 movement works to raise the minimum wage to $15 an hour, one of the unintended consequences will be the deployment of automation and robots. I am already seeing fast-food chains rolling out mobile apps and kiosks where you can order your food and never have to speak to a person. I am seeing lots of requests from career middle managers in the retail segment looking for assistance in getting out of the industry.

Hopefully, I have demonstrated to you that even professions that seem immune to automation and robots are at risk. Similarly, if the industry where you are working is at risk, you must be on the lookout. If you think you are safe from automation and robots sabotaging your career, you must be smoking something, and you *are* inhaling.

CAREER DISASTER AREA

It is devastating when the career you've built, the skills you honed, that seniority you have acquired, have all been wiped out because somebody built a robot that can do what you do faster and cheaper, if not better. For many people, these changes have hit like an earthquake or a hurricane. They are living in a "Career Disaster Area." They will recover, but they won't be moving back into the old house.

My client Sally was the consummate marketing professional. She had worked in various industries over her career, both as a freelancer and as an employee for major agencies.

Like many of her peers, she took a hit in the great recession, and then her spouse passed away suddenly. At 65, Sally decided to move across the country to be closer to her children. Now she is trying to reestablish herself in a new city, where the culture and job market are very young and vibrant. Sally is taking courses in social media and digital marketing, but the skills required to be a productive marketing professional have made tectonic shifts in the direction of technology and analytics.

In the 1990s, when I was working in the marketing and sales support function either in IBM marketing or in an executive briefing center, we produced presentations, marketing collateral, and web content that supported the sale of IBM hardware and software. Much of that world is gone.

The world that exists today, as I launch the Career Pivot online community, requires a completely new set of skills. Much of the content produced today falls into the arena of brand journalism; brands have become media sites. To promote Career Pivot I am learning about Facebook marketing, Google AdWords, remarketing and pixeling strategies, ad networks, and other digital marketing approaches. When I left the world of technology marketing more than 15 years ago, I left a place that looks NOTHING like it does today.

Can Sally shift into this new technological marketing world with a very young workforce?

It is not probable.

Larry is also 65. He is an engineer who has worked for some of the top companies that designed and manufactured leading computer hardware. He was a program and project manager for multi-national and multi-company development projects with huge scope and complexity.

That world is disappearing fast. **HP, IBM and others** have seen their hardware businesses evaporate. Companies like **Sun** and **DEC** have been wiped off the map. Instead, companies use a combination of cloud-based services and nimble apps.

There are many like Larry who built their careers around designing large and ever-growing, complex hardware systems. But in the last 10 years, the hardware market has become commoditized. The iPhone sitting next to me has more computing power and function than huge computers of just a few years ago.

Larry interviewed for a program management job with one of the leading cloud infrastructure companies. The first thing they asked him to do was take a coding test. WHAT? A coding test? For a program management job?

Like Larry, I have not written a line of code in over 15 years. Could I pass a coding test? Probably not. Does it make sense that they want to see if he can code? Probably not. But that is not the world we live in now.

THEY MOVED MY CHEESE!

The complex world that Larry thrived in moved from hardware to software at warp speed. They moved Larry's cheese and he did not even realize it. The career space that Larry and his peers lived in for so many years now looks like a Career Disaster Area. Like Sally, he could retool. But can he do it fast enough and be accepted in a very young, fast-moving market?

It is not probable.

It is now time to shift expectations and direction.

People rebuild after disasters. Sometimes they are forced to leave the disaster scene because it is too risky to stay. This is the destruction part. But after a period of grieving, it's time to move away from the destruction and get on with the creation.

From here on out, there is no safe haven where you can just tuck yourself in and work as long as you want to work. Creative destruction is happening every day. You have to be constantly learning, evolving, and pivoting. How to do that is the subject of the next chapter.

ACTION STEPS

✓ Is your industry being SMAC'd? Evaluate whether you're keeping up with the changes.

✓ Research what skills you need to keep up with your current industry and how much of a challenge that would be. Does it mean going back to school or merely taking some online classes?

✓ Write down how your current skills might be useful in other, emerging business types or industries.

For additional resources, check out the Repurpose Your Career Resource Center at CareerPivot.com/RYC-Resources.

.

CREATE OPPORTUNITIES AND STOP REACTING

Creative destruction means that anywhere, at any time, someone could invent a technology that does your work better than you do. Or they could introduce a business model that renders your company obsolete. Or consumer tastes could change, making your product irrelevant. Even if you can find someone to hire you, there's no guarantee that company will be around—or require your skill set—a few years from now.

Growing up, most of us were taught to look for opportunities that others created for us—i.e. job openings. Many of us think of things in a linear way: "Now I'm doing this; when this appears to be drawing to a close, I'll find the next thing." That's a strategy for a slower time. I have talked with a variety of individuals who are busy running around, applying to jobs, and getting very frustrated. All of these individuals are over 50 and refuse to see the world has changed.

Today you never know where the next force of creative destruction will come from, or the next opportunity. You need to network strategically, and pay attention to what's happening in your industry, your town, your culture. You must be prepared to create your own opportunities, over and over again, to shift from one set of skills to another, and from one way of providing value to another, as technology and circumstances change. A lot of people don't want to do all that hustling at this point in their careers. Well, too bad. That's the world of work today. You may have colleagues who are already doing this. They seem to effortlessly flow from one new venture to the next. So how do they do it? And how do you create new opportunities for yourself?

LOOK FOR A PROBLEM TO SOLVE

You sure don't do it by sitting still like a turkey, waiting for something to happen. You don't need to look for a job someone else created for you. You need to look for a problem to solve.

Look at your own experience, your network, your community, your world and see what problems need solving. *That's* how you create an opportunity. This is an entrepreneurial mindset that puts you in charge of your own career.

A client of mine with piloting expertise realized that the drone piloting business was brand new and there was a lot of demand. He quickly became an expert and opened his own drone services company. My image consultant realized there was a need for earrings that didn't make older women's earlobes sag. She created a business to buy and sell them. Next Avenue, a public media website for people in the second half of life, wrote about some Baby Boomers who saw that Millennials and Generation Z were afraid of "adulting" because they lacked basic skills. So, they started an adulting school to teach things like sewing, cooking, and money management. That's what I mean by looking for problems to solve.

I recently spoke with a 70-year-old former tech pro who had been retired for 18 years and whose nest egg was disappearing. He assumed he needed to go find a J-O-B in the technology world. But his professional network was largely gone, and his technical skills were obsolete.

His most valuable skills acquired over the last 18 years have been the engineering things he has done on his own property. When I told him to find a problem to solve, that got him juiced. He immediately started talking about an issue that he had with his water well pump, and the solution he had been working on. His entrepreneurial pump was primed. This could turn into a business, a product, consulting gig, or a job. Since his tech skills have atrophied, he's like Thomas Wolfe's character George Webber: He can't go home again. He needs to start creating opportunities in completely new places.

For many of you, this will be a frightening thought, but you may find it very empowering. Creative destruction creates opportunities.

- Write and publish books. Check out Mark Dawson's Self-Publishing Formula site to learn how to publish your own books. I have no affiliation other than I listen to the *SPF* podcast.

- Record audiobooks. Use a service like ACX.com to record the books yourself, or you can find voice talent to record the book for you.

- Become a Virtual Assistant. You get to use your skills, set your schedule and your rates, and work from anywhere in the world.

- Buy things to sell on Amazon as a reseller.

- Build an online business where you teach anything to anyone in the world. I belong to a community called the **Flipped LifeStyle,** where I am building the Career Pivot community.

- Work remotely as a full-time or part-time, freelancer.

- Drive. Be a rideshare driver or deliver food or packages.

- Rent out a room in your house as a short-term rental or as storage. Recently, we traveled to Ecuador and stayed at an Airbnb managed by an American who rented the property from a local dentist. He then listed it on Airbnb as a short-term rental. This was how he supported himself.

One of my clients, David, is 68 and ex-military. He spent much of his career in policy positions in state and local government. His career was basically a series of assignments where he was sent to solve a problem, spent a few years creating a policy to do so, and left after three to five years, either because the problem was solved or because the system responsible for the problem was so rigid he couldn't fix it. Next, he became the CEO of a small association for real-estate agents, which was a horrible job for him because the culture of real-estate agents is the absolute opposite of what he was used to in government service.

I would have assumed, since he has worked in war zones, he was comfortable with risk. I was wrong. When we started talking about creating opportunities, it turned out that he was very risk-averse, and that one of the things we would have to work on was creating opportunities for him to take small risks. He began teaching a class online at a state university, launched a consulting practice, and took a job working part time at a Small Business Development Center (SBDC). At the

SBDC, he would have the chance to meet with lots of entrepreneurs who had ideas that he might be able to draw from for his own ongoing career journey.

Another person I spoke to is a dean at a public university. Like many people in the academic world, he is going to have a struggle shifting into the private sector. People in academia are used to having a lot of freedom, like summers off for private pursuits. He will have to use his network to figure out which of his skills are needed in the private sector and how much he can charge for them.

For most people, the answer is not in moving into one job, but creating different opportunities with different skill sets to create an income portfolio. That might mean having one main role with side gigs, which is what many Millennials do.

SAFE IS THE NEW RISKY

People create new opportunities every day. These opportunities do not look like the safe choices we expected earlier in our career. **Playing it safe is the new risky.** I started the planning process for Career Pivot in early 2009. Incorporation occurred in late 2010, and the Career Pivot brand was launched in February 2012. I had thought things through, gotten advice from many trusted

113

advisers, and hired a coach. In 2012, on a Sunday afternoon, I had a phone conversation with my coach.

I told her that I was feeling very anxious about a variety of things. Logically, I knew everything was going according to plan, but I was a wreck emotionally. She reminded me that I had remade myself many times before. (This was my seventh career change of some sort in 35 years.) Why was this any different? I told her it was not. Every time I go through these changes, it stirs up a lot of anxiety. I perceived emotionally that I was taking a big risk. It was my perception and, therefore, it was my reality. I was not playing it safe! But the truth is, playing it safe is being a turkey.

Odds are, you're going to have to evolve how you make money and where you invest your time over and over. Just getting good at creating opportunities for yourself is the most valuable and reliable skill set you'll need for the second half of your life.

So, what problems do you see that need solving?

ACTION STEPS

✓ Look for a problem to solve. Look all through your life, not just in your career or industry area. It could be that a problem you need solved is something someone else needs a solution to as well.

✓ Let go of the idea of a job and start thinking in terms of creating opportunities for yourself. Don't just think of one; think of several. What would be the path to getting started?

For additional resources, check out the Repurpose Your Career Resource Center at CareerPivot.com/RYC-Resources

LIFE AS A SQUARE PEG GETS TOUGHER AS YOU AGE

When you go to work, you have to play a role. The closer that role is to who you authentically are, the happier you are likely to be. But to one extent or another, we all have to be actors at our jobs to fit into the culture. We behave in the way we believe our bosses and our team expect us to behave. Many business cultures:

- Show little value for, or interest in, music, art, or literature.

- Expect employees to follow the rules.

- Reward employees for being extroverted.

- Want you to check emotions at the door.

- Value strong and engaged leadership.

Some, or all, of these things might be at odds with how you naturally function. When you're younger, it seems easier to be an actor at work. You've probably been playing a role all your life—in school, on teams, with peers. But the older you get, the more exhausting it is to put on the show. At some point, after decades of acting, building experience, proving yourself, adapting to new cast members, you just want to say, "I can't be bothered. Just let me do what I'm good at and leave me alone." You don't want to pretend to be interested in things you're not interested in that aren't relevant to getting the job done. You don't want your boss practicing strong, engaged leadership on you when you know your job better than they do.

This is especially hard when you're a square peg in a round hole. And a lot of people are square pegs.

Sometimes they're square pegs because their personality doesn't lend itself to the social dynamic of the workplace. This is my situation. I'm an introvert, but I have to act the role of an extrovert to succeed in the work world.

Sometimes they're square pegs because the culture of their particular industry doesn't really fit them as a person, like an engineer who is highly emotionally intelligent.

Sometimes they came to this job from another country and everything about this culture requires them to behave in a way that's different from how they grew up behaving.

I have been working with quite a few square pegs. They just do not fit into the traditional roles that are defined by their organizations. Some try to squeeze themselves into those roles. But even when they succeed, they usually wind up being unhappy and unhealthy. The stress of making themselves fit wreaks havoc on their physical and mental health.

PERSONALITY SQUARE PEGS

As an introvert acting the part of an extrovert, I used to be able to stay in character for a long time, back in my 20s, 30s, and 40s. But when I reached my 50s, staying in character became exhausting. Periodically I would be completely depleted, which was not at all how people knew me. And it would take a long time to recharge. The more I allowed myself to get completely drained, the longer it took to recharge.

Our society is biased toward extroverts. Extroverts make more money. They're taken more seriously as leaders. They're perceived as more competent, even though, as Susan Cain pointed out in her book *Quiet: The Power of Introverts in a World That Can't Stop Talking*, many of our great thinkers and artists have been introverts.

That's only one kind of square peg. There are others:

CREATIVE

Creative people have a very high interest in music, art, and/or literature. Many creatives have abandoned those interests because they do not fit into what our economy values or is willing to pay for. Instead, these people often express their creativity in colorful spreadsheets or attractive PowerPoint presentations.

AUTONOMOUS

Autonomous people do not like staying between the lines. They want the freedom to do it their own way. They are good in chaotic situations where they get to make decisions.

HIGH EMPATHY

People with high empathy treat people with kindness and caring and want their colleagues to treat them the same way. I have worked in the high-tech field for most of my career. High empathy people are not generally welcomed or considered the norm.

LOW AUTHORITY

People who do not embrace authority would prefer having a colleague to a boss. If you try to micromanage them, it is not pretty!

These personality traits are largely incompatible with today's work environment.

INDUSTRY OR COMPANY MISMATCH
SQUARE PEGS

THE PROJECT MANAGER

I worked with a client who was a top-flight IT project manager. Her boss would give her a project, she'd run it for a year, and then her boss would give her another project just like it. This was a dream scenario for a lot of project managers, but it was not at all what she had in mind. She wanted to be constantly learning new things and tackling new challenges so she could grow and develop in her career. But every year, at the end of the project, here came another project just like the one she had just finished. Finally, she complained, and her boss was taken aback.

"But," they said, "we're putting you in your comfort zone."

That was the last place she wanted to be.

THE MUSICAL TECHNOLOGIST

I have met multiple musical technologists over the last few years. It is very common for engineers to have high interests in music.

Recently I was speaking with a gentleman I will call Ron who works for a very large hospital system. He evaluates systems and must stay on top of all technologies the hospital is implementing.

With the advent of Electronic Medical Records and all of the downstream technologies, the rate of change has accelerated.

At the same time, Ron has a huge interest in music that he has relegated to the side for many years to raise a family, pay off the mortgage, and put his kids through college. Ron can keep up with the technological changes—but he does not want to. What once was fun, interesting and lot of work is now just a lot of work.

He has spent the last few years taking care of elderly parents. His priorities have shifted.

Ron spent years shoving the square peg of himself into the technology round hole.

THE CREATIVE TECHNOLOGIST

This last example is Sam, who wandered into technology a long time ago. He did not really select it, but it was there at the time he graduated from college.

Over the last 20 years, he has worked in the IT departments of large companies. He has gotten pretty good at it. Today he is in IT security, which is a hot area. The problem is he is sick of it. He is both mentally and physically tired.

Now that Sam is in his mid to late 50s, he can no longer keep shoving his square peg into the round hole of his job. He is physically fit and can do it. But he does not want to anymore.

Sam is highly creative and would love to marry his technical knowledge with some form of art. He is now exploring different video options with virtual and augmented reality. The big question is whether he can he make a go of this AND keep putting his kids through college at the same time.

CULTURAL DYSLEXIA SQUARE PEGS

Another issue I see is cultural dyslexia. These are people born into an indirect culture (Indian, Chinese, Japanese, etc.) but who then spent their teenage years in a direct culture (such as that of the U.S. and Europe). They attend Western universities and acquire some Western personality traits.

The problem is that they do not feel they belong in either their birth culture or their adopted culture. I call this cultural dyslexia, and we will see a lot more of this issue as people move around the world.

Does everyone who makes this transition suffer from cultural dyslexia? No! However, I have seen it enough to know it causes people who have it great angst as they try to fit in that round hole.

SQUARE PEGS AND FINANCIAL REQUIREMENTS FOR THE SECOND HALF OF LIFE

I was quite blessed that my first tech startup left us debt free in my late 40s. We had children in our late 20s—early by today's standards. Many of the square pegs I have talked with lately chose to delay starting families until their careers were established. Spending your late 50s or early 60s putting children through college is not unusual.

Many of us have lived through two horrible recessions that decimated both retirement and our kids' college savings. Many square pegs feel they have no choice but to stay unhappily and uncomfortably in their ill-fitting niche.

This is one reason my wife and I moved to Mexico. We enjoy a lower cost of living and a slower pace of life—and I can continue to avoid that damn round career hole. But for many people, the task is to define and find their own unique career hole.

Let me show you my process for helping square pegs find their unique career hole.

DEFINE YOUR CAREER HOLE

Another way to put this is: *know thyself.*

You cannot target your ideal working environment unless you know what it is. You cannot find your unique career hole if you cannot define it.

Can you clearly articulate what your ideal work environment looks like? For 99 percent of you, the answer is a resounding NO.

Reflect upon when you have been happy in seven different areas during your career:

Boss: When did you have a boss you really liked? What made that person a good boss for you?

Team: When did you have a really great team? What was the makeup of that team?

Rewards: When did you feel valued at work? What made you feel valued?

Structure: How much structure do you need at work, and who should create that structure?

Variety: How much variety do you need within your day?

Emotions: Do you need a supportive, emotional environment at work?

Activity: How much activity do you need during your day?

Use my career reflection worksheet in the resource center to help you.

Once you have clearly defined when things were really good, reflect on times when things were really bad. I use the <u>Birkman Assessment</u> to help my clients identify situations that cause them stress and, determine how to avoid them.

Now we can clearly identify the shape of your unique career hole. *We can start the search!*

LOCATING YOUR UNIQUE CAREER HOLE

Next, create a list of open-ended questions such as:

- Will you tell me about your management style?

- How much freedom will I have in determining my schedule?

- What does a typical workday look like at your company?

- How do you make your employees feel valued?

The next step is to target companies within your industry or profession that can hire you. You will dutifully use your questions to determine which companies have a unique career hole that matches your requirements. This is not easy! It takes a great deal of tenacity and patience.

For some square pegs, it means going to work for themselves. For others, it means working for smaller organizations that are willing to create unique career holes for them.

Do you know the shape of your unique career hole? Are you ready to define it?

FIND RESTORATIVE NICHES

I appear to be an extrovert because I am a great public speaker, I can work a networking event with the best of them, and I can meet and mingle with strangers with ease. When I am done, I am exhausted.

This did not happen overnight. In my 22 years at IBM, I slowly became an articulate techno-weenie; a geek who could speak. I was paid more and more money to do this.

When I hit my late 30s and early 40s, my back would spasm once or more times a year. I would be down for a week or more. Finally, my L4/L5 discs ruptured, and after taking three months off for bed rest, I kept going. Now that I am over 60, I have to be careful how much public speaking I do.

Like other square pegs, I have to learn to take time to recover. One recent Saturday I gave a workshop for the employees of a Dallas bank about working in a multigenerational company. The drive to Dallas from Austin is three hours. I spent the time listening to podcasts. Then I gave the two-hour workshop and drove back home. The time in the car provided restorative niches.

I have to allow a lot of alone time before and after being around people or I will be dead the rest of the day. Even though I am really good at being around people and presenting workshops, I am a square peg and shoving myself into that round hole is EXHAUSTING, especially now that I am older.

A restorative niche might be putting on your headphones and listening to your favorite music while you work, doing creative projects in your spare time, or spending time in nature.

As I said in the beginning, pretty much every job requires you to play a role. Even if you work for yourself, you have to play a role with your customers or clients. But the closer your role is to who you really are, the happier you'll be.

ACTION STEPS

✓ Are you a square peg? Write down what roles you have been playing throughout your career that you would like to stop playing now.

✓ Write down some of your personal square peg attributes and how they could be useful in different jobs/businesses. How can you find a way to work around them where necessary?

✓ Write down some questions you could ask an employer that would help you see how well you and the organization's culture would fit.

For additional resources, check out the Repurpose Your Career Resource Center at CareerPivot.com/RYC-Resources

.

IF YOU WANT TO WORK INTO YOUR 70S

Do you want to work in your 70s? I know that seems like a weird concept, but I want to work into my 70s, though I don't want a traditional job. I want to work on my own terms, doing something I love.

I once heard Geoff Pearman of Partners in Change say: "In your 50s, start thinking about what you want to do for work for the next 20 years."

It dawned on me that this is a big shift from what many of us expected to be thinking about in our 50s. We expected to be planning our retirement. But we're going to live a lot longer than the generation before us. Also, it turns out retirement can be really boring. So, more and more people I meet want to be working into their 70s. But they're not up for 20 more years of daily grind. In fact, when they talk about their work, they share some common themes:

- Freedom to work on their terms

- Having work they enjoy

- Doing work they find meaningful

129

That set of priorities is a 180-degree difference from where most of us started our careers.

But it is hard to imagine what our work will be. The world is changing so fast; it will be very different in 20 years than it is now. Creative destruction has transformed communications, supply chain, sales, medicine, transportation, lodging, marketing, technology, management, and more. It seems like anybody's guess how we might be living in 20 years and what will be needed. It is fairly easy to presume, though, that you won't have full-time employment. Instead, your future might be a part-time job, multiple part-time jobs, freelance work, or a full-blown portfolio career.

In thinking about your future career, it's good to ask yourself:

- Will you *have to work* in your 70s? If so, how much money do you think you will need to make?

- Do you want to work for yourself or someone else?

- If you want to work for yourself, are you prepared to sell and market your services or products?

The answers will vary for everyone.

WILL YOU HAVE TO WORK INTO YOUR 70S?

Knowing the real answer to this is key, and probably will require help from a financial advisor. Very few can figure this out on their own. When I left my last corporate gig in 2011, I went to my financial advisor and asked the question, can I retire? The answer was yes.

This is because my wife and I live a modest lifestyle, have no debt, own our home/condo, and have no intentions of changing any of those things. We also have saved money for years and did not change our investment strategies during the last two recessions. I'm a fan of two finance podcasts:

- *The Retirement Answer Man*

- *Money Matters* by Allworth Financial

Listening to these podcasts can give you good insights about how to think of your financial future.

DO YOU WANT TO WORK FOR YOURSELF OR SOMEONE ELSE?

I will never forget the response Bruce Williams gave a caller back in the 1980s. Someone asked the nationally syndicated radio host, who spoke on business and money, whether it was better to work for themselves or for someone else. Bruce responded that some people can work for themselves and others have to work for someone else, and there is no right or wrong. That response has stuck with me to this day.

In my last corporate gig, I worked for a person who was the closest thing to a sociopath I had ever experienced. That job left me exhausted, and I told myself I would never work for someone else again. But I now work for a jerk! Well, I do work for myself. My boss always knows when I'm:

- Goofing off

- Faking illness

- Procrastinating

- Running late on a project

Despite all that, he has given up trying to fire me. Working for myself, I've had to learn a lot of key skills. For example:

Delegate: As a solo-entrepreneur, it is easy to tell yourself that you should do it all. This is a myth. I now have a bookkeeper, an editor, an intern for social media, a webmaster, a virtual assistant, and various co-authors.

Automate: I have automated parts of my business by using low-cost or free tools for much of my social media, calendar, email, and website.

My boss let me take a vacation this year. This was the first real vacation my wife and I have taken in several years! I have been on this entrepreneurial journey more than five years and working for myself has not been easy. From the beginning, maintaining a healthy work-life balance has been really difficult. This was especially true in the early years when money was tight, and it was not clear whether my business would thrive.

It was really challenging, figuring out how to promote what I was doing, building relationships, working hard to take care of clients, and selling my services. Though what I was doing often spoke directly to what people were going through, we had to overcome the hurdle that they had never heard of a business like mine.

And that brings up the next question ...

IF YOU WANT TO WORK INTO YOUR 70S AND WORK FOR YOURSELF, ARE YOU PREPARED TO SELL?

Selling has changed. A lot. People do their own research online for the products and services they need, and they often won't take you seriously until they run across your name, over and over again, as the solution. It's not about direct sales. It's about relationships and doing such a good job that your customers bring in more customers. It's a lot of work, and you can't be shy about it

When I began this journey, a friend recommended I read the book *Getting Naked: A Business Fable About Shedding The Three Fears That Sabotage Client Loyalty* by Patrick Lencioni. It is a story about consultative selling and defines a process that most of us can use. "Getting naked" is being vulnerable to a new client. You walk in without all the answers and listen. The goal is to see if you can help.

START EXPLORING

It may take some time to figure out what is right for you. It may be a combination of things. The point is to get started and explore. Will some paths take you to a dead end? Probably.

When they do, go back and start over, but take the knowledge you have gained with you. I have failed multiple times and learned from each experience.

Will this take longer than you think? Probably.

Do not let that deter you from finding the right path.

ACTION STEPS

✓ Look into your future. Do you want to work into your 70s? Do you *need* to work into your 70s? If you were going to work into your 70s, write down some specifics about the kind of work would you like to do and will be able to do.

✓ Examine your skill sets, interests, needs, and personality. Can you think of a problem you could solve using skills you already have?

✓ Consider obstacles you may run up against that you need to plan for—health, time, resources. What are some strategies for tackling those?

For additional resources, check out the Repurpose Your Career Resource Center at CareerPivot.com/RYC-Resources

PLAYBOOK FOR BUILDING STRATEGIC RELATIONSHIPS

Often when I talk about strategic networking, people think I'm talking about going to networking events. Their palms get sweaty, and they start thinking of excuses, since most people would rather get root canal surgery than walk into a room full of strangers.

So now I talk about building strategic relationships instead. In reality, people don't build relationships at networking events. Relationships form after the event, when you sit down and meet one on one. You get to know one another and find common ground.

With whom should you build this type of strategic relationship?

CONNECTORS

Connectors are people who know a lot of people and enjoy connecting them. You can recognize connectors by the fact that they are always introducing people to each other, either in person or via email or social media, suggesting ways they could be helpful to each other.

I am a connector. I know a lot of people and thoroughly enjoy playing matchmaker.

Don't rely too much on one connector, or you will wear out your relationship. They'll end up feeling like they work for you—for no pay. That's why you need several connectors in your network.

Another important thing about connectors is that they are not just in it for you. They serve as connectors for many people, all of whom matter to them. They will introduce you to people who can help you find work or clients, but they will also introduce others to you, expecting you to help. Be sure to respond and provide help as well as receiving it.

There is a special class of connector called a recruiter. You should carefully cultivate strategic relationships with recruiters. They are very busy people, but they are "people people." Whenever you engage with them, do it with a purpose and state that purpose clearly.

MENTORS

As a Baby Boomer who started my career at IBM in the 1970s, I was never encouraged to find mentors. Still, I knew I needed people who could advise me about my career, who really knew what they were talking about, and who weren't jerks! There were some people with really big egos; they would not help anyone. But there were others you could learn from. Seek those people out and cultivate formal mentoring relationships.

I now have multiple mentors in different subject areas.

INDUSTRY OR COMPANY EXPERT

Whom in your industry or company do you need to know? Be very selective and make sure they know who you are and what value you bring to the table. You do not need to form a bond with these people, but you do need to be on their radar screen.

I have a client who works for a company that is downsizing. My client is working to maintain "his seat" until he can move on. When the last round of layoffs came, my client went to a person of importance within the company and asked for advice. The person of importance could assure my client of nothing, but we found out later that the person of importance stepped in to make sure my client had "his seat." That relationship was built several years earlier!

PEERS

This may sound odd, but seek out peers and see how you can help them. It is important to help others and expect nothing in return. Be that person people know they can turn to when they need help.

Locate the LinkedIn profile of everyone you know who could be part of your tribe. You may want to build an Excel spreadsheet and categorize each contact.

- Connectors

- Mentors

- Company or Industry Experts

- Peers

It may take you a week or more to think of every person and then categorize them. But this will give you an idea about the strength of your network, and how to strategically build it. Once you've categorized everyone, look at your network! What role does everyone play in your success? What strategic relationships are missing? What do you need more of? Do you have too few connectors? Too few company or industry experts? Do you have one or more mentors? Do you need a mentor in a particular skill area?

Develop a list of people you would like to meet. Who in your network knows them well enough to make an introduction? I always want an introduction to a new connection. Think of this in sales terminology as a warm lead.

STRATEGIC NETWORKING MEANS BUILDING YOUR TRIBE

Do you have a tribe—people you can go to for a favor and actually expect it to be granted? Dig through your e-mail contacts, LinkedIn connections, and Facebook friends, and identify people you'd feel comfortable asking for help. For many of us, this is a very short list. But we're not necessarily talking "help me move" kind of help. It might just be getting together for coffee to discuss strategies for infiltrating a company you're interested in working for.

Not everyone is in your tribe. You may have 10,000 followers on Twitter or 5,000 connections on LinkedIn, but how many do you really know? The number of relationships you can maintain is known as the Dunbar number. Evolutionary psychologist Robin Dunbar studied the Christmas-card-sending habits of the English and found that they sent on average 153.5 cards each year. The number of 150 has come up over and over in society. The Amish break up communities when they reach 150. Chimpanzee families reach a maximum of 150.

A tribe goes beyond "people you know." These are people who understand what you're aiming for and are in your corner. If they meet someone who needs what you're offering, they'll make an introduction. They actually want to know how it's going in your life, your career, and your job hunt. They're not just being polite. Your tribe will also turn to you when they need help, advice, or a referral. A tribe is like the old barn-raisings where you'd show up with your tools to help a neighbor build his barn, knowing he'll show up to help build yours.

When I worked as an algebra teacher at an inner-city high school, I struggled. I struggled with the job of teaching. I struggled with how to help kids, many of whom came from difficult backgrounds and definitely did not arrive ready to learn. I struggled with being a novice after years of being an expert.

Every three weeks I sent an e-mail to a list of about 100 people. I wrote about my students. I shared the difficulties I was having, the funny things the kids said, the triumphs and the frustrations. And to my surprise, the readers really responded. They looked forward to the emails. They shared them with other people. They gave me encouraging feedback. In short, they became my fan club and my tribe. I received lots of advice and help, but more importantly, I received love and support. I would not have made it through my first year of teaching without my tribe!

Do you have 150 in your tribe? If the answer is no, you have some work to do. Is there an area where you are weak or have too few connections?

Leverage your network to help you develop those strategic relationships! Once you have an introduction, schedule either a meeting over coffee or, if they are not local, on the phone.

If you make one outreach a week, your tribe will grow naturally and strategically.

CULTIVATING YOUR TRIBE

You have to cultivate your tribe like a garden. From time to time, you need to weed it of people you have no real connection with. You have to water it when there's no rain. You may need to apply fertilizer. Most importantly, you can't neglect it. It needs regular TLC. It needs to be part of the way you think and live, or it will wither.

Do you have friends you only hear from when they want something? One of the easiest ways to provide TLC for your tribe is to stay in touch. Do you have friends you have not seen in months?

At least once a week, I glance through LinkedIn or Outlook contacts and find someone I have not heard from in a while. I send them an email as simple as:

Bob,

Haven't heard from you in a while. How are you doing? How is your family? Things are going well with my business. Son getting married and they make a great couple. Wife's business is still slow but getting better.

Let me know how you're doing. Do you want to meet for coffee soon?

Marc

I almost always get a response like the following:

Marc,

Thanks for checking in with me. Life is good. Too busy to meet for coffee right now, but check back in.

Bob

I now know how he is doing, and he knows that I care about him. Cultivating is all about building relationships.

Messages are helpful, but there is no substitute for a face-to-face meeting where you get to shake hands and read body language. I like to have coffee meetings first thing in the morning. When our son was small, I learned that it was easy for me to protect that hour. Others could schedule things for me to do the rest of the day, but first thing in the morning was sacred.

Sometimes I meet a new contact for a morning walk instead of coffee. What time works for you? Lunch? After work for a beer or other libation? Or maybe Saturdays? Schedule a time to regularly meet face to face with someone in your network. Make it a habit!

And when you meet with this person, make sure you're building relationship, rather than killing it. Frequently, when people use their contacts to try to change careers, they make one of these three mistakes:

1. They spend the whole time talking about themselves.

2. They spend the whole time asking questions the other person doesn't feel comfortable answering.

3. They squander the interview and forget to meet their primary objectives.

How you present yourself to the people who are helping you furthers your personal brand. If you make one or more of the mistakes I just mentioned, then you communicate that your personal brand is self-centered, unprofessional, or scattered. But if you're focused, clear and appropriate, that's what your interviewee is going to remember. Let's say you are looking for a new position. You want to check out this hot new startup. You did your homework and received an introduction to one of the managers, Natalie. Do you ask Natalie for an informational interview? No. Here's what to do instead.

ASK FOR A-I-R

A=Advice: When you ask for advice, it is a compliment. Rarely will anyone ever turn you down when you ask for advice. In an e-mail to Natalie, ask for 30 minutes of her time to ask for some advice. It could be about how to pursue a position at the company or to learn more about the company. The magic word is "advice"!

I=Insights: Once you meet Natalie, ask for her insights into how the company functions, the culture, and management structure. You might ask her how she was hired or what she likes or doesn't like about her job. Ask very open-ended questions to give her space and time to talk. This is NOT ABOUT YOU.

R=Recommendations: This is the part that many people forget. Ask "what should I do next?" "Is there anyone else you would recommend I talk with?" "Can you introduce me to anyone else within the organization?"

Remember, talk about yourself only when asked! This is all about building the relationship. Asking for advice, insight, and recommendations is a great way to initiate and cultivate a lasting relationship.

You have not asked for help to get a job. You have asked for help in understanding the organization, and for further networking opportunities. You are networking to build relationships and not to find a job. The opportunity to interview for a position will come after you have established relationships.

Natalie will likely introduce you to at least one person if you made it clear you were interested in her insight and perspective. You can then ask for advice, insights and recommendations from each person Natalie introduced you to.

When each of those meetings is complete, who are you gonna call? Natalie.

Well, maybe not call, but at least send her an e-mail and let her know how it went. You will also tell her if you received any more introductions. People love to know that they're helping and that the time they spent with you had some value. They also appreciate knowing that you're grateful and recognize the time and effort they contributed to your career search.

Now, if a position opens up at this hot startup, Natalie will think of you. If you made a favorable impression, she might even call you before the position is posted. I was hired exactly this way at my last two tech startup companies.

INCLUDE RECRUITERS IN YOUR TRIBE

Recruiters are an integral part of the hiring process at most companies. There are several things you need to understand about them.

- They are people who like dealing with people. Most recruiters became recruiters because they are social and like helping others. In general, they are very nice people.

- They change jobs frequently. With the ups and downs of the economy, recruiters are the first to be laid off when things get bad and the first to be hired when things turn around.

- They connect with almost everyone in the organizations they work for and carry those connections from company to company. They have large networks.

- A recruiter is often the person between you and the hiring manager.

- If there's anyone you want to share your personal brand with, it's recruiters.

When you locate a company that looks like a good potential employer for your services, you should do the following: Go to LinkedIn search and look on the title field for "recruiter". I use the following search string: "recruiter OR Talent OR Human Resources OR HR." Some organizations do not use "recruiter" in their titles or may not have someone in HR dedicated to recruiting. Also try "talent acquisition specialist." Identify recruiters and send them connection requests that state why you want to connect. Here's an example:

Dear (insert recruiters name,)

I am very interested in a marketing position at XYZ company (if there is a current position open mention it.) Are you the recruiter who handles these kinds of positions? If not, could you direct me to the recruiter who does? Could we set up a time to talk about your organization? In the meantime, please accept this invitation to connect.

Your name

When the recruiter receives your invitation, three things are likely to happen:

1. They will look at your profile. That is your #1 goal! If you have LinkedIn Premium you will be able to see who looked at your profile by monitoring the section called Who's Viewed Your Profile. Sometimes you can see some people who have looked at your profile even without premium.

2. Almost every time, the recruiters will accept your invitation. You will now rise higher in their searches because you are a first-degree connection. And their networks of company employees are now your second-degree connections, and you can see full names of employees in the target company!

3. If they like your profile, they will likely reach out to you for a short conversation via e-mail or over the phone. They may forward you on to the recruiter who handles the positions you are looking for.

If they don't connect, try a different recruiter at the same company.

But if the recruiter does connect, call them. Here's what to say:

- If you are looking at a specific job, ask which recruiter is handling the position.

- If you are looking at a specific area within the company, ask which recruiter is handling that specific area.

- Ask about the culture and opportunities within the company.

If the recruiter does not answer, leave a message with your questions and follow up with an email.

Be persistent and repeat this procedure in a few days if you don't get a response.

If they accept your connection but you never hear from them, send them an e-mail or LinkedIn message.

Recruiters need you as much as you need them. They are looking for referrals. When you talk with them, always be polite and courteous. Always complete the conversation with "How can I help you?"

Remember that recruiters move around. Keep track of their career moves using LinkedIn. Be helpful to them when you are not looking for the next gig. I cannot stress enough that building long-term relationships with recruiters will pay long-term dividends.

One last tip about recruiters: They'll usually use a company email address on LinkedIn. From their address, you can figure out how the company formats email addresses (for example, jane.doe@company.com or jdoe@company.com). This helps you guess the emails of other employees you may want to contact.

You next career move will likely come through a relationship. Are you ready to cultivate and manage that relationship strategically? You now have a playbook for strategic networking. Are you ready to execute the plays?

ACTION STEPS

✓ Make a spreadsheet of people you consider your tribe. How many are connectors, peers, industry experts, recruiters? Are you missing anyone from your tribe?

✓ Begin connecting with people from the categories you've listed where you're currently missing connections.

✓ Cultivate your tribe by doing the work to build relationships. Schedule time each week to reach out to people in your tribe and ask how they are, offer help, or ask to meet for coffee or a walk.

For additional resources, check out the Repurpose Your Career Resource Center at CareerPivot.com/RYC-Resources

BUILDING ON WEAK TIES

When people think about who might help them in a job search, they tend to make a very short list, along the lines of people you might ask to help you move: very close friends, people who owe you a favor. That's actually a big mistake.

In 1973, Johns Hopkins sociologist Mark Granovetter wrote a paper called "The Strength of Weak Ties." Malcom Gladwell brought this paper to the world's attention in his book *The Tipping Point*. Granovetter was exploring the relationships we have with people we know slightly or by reputation, but with whom we are not close. He called them our weak ties. Granovetter postulated that we might actually be more influenced by people with whom we have weak ties than by those with whom we have strong ties. If your best friend buys a pair of bright orange shoes, for example, you might think it's crazy. But if you suddenly start seeing several people wearing bright orange shoes, your perspective might shift, and you start to think "This is a trend. I should get some bright orange shoes."

Granovetter was talking about the distribution of ideas, but the same thing works with behavior. If your partner tells you your sense of humor is inappropriate, for example, you might just think "Oh, they're picking on me again." But if someone you only know distantly through business tells you the same thing, you'll probably give the criticism a lot more weight.

When you communicate with those with whom you have strong ties, you use a kind of shorthand. They know you are unhappy in your job, or out of work, or having financial issues—there is no need to provide background information.

When you communicate with those you know less well you must be much more explicit. You need to state exactly what you want and why. Sometimes this can force you to articulate even for yourself what you need.

A great explanation from the "Changing Minds" website says:

In the familiarity of strong ties we use simple restricted codes, where much is implicit and taken for granted. In communicating through the weak ties, we need more explicit elaborated codes for meaning to be fully communicated. When elaborating, we have more scope for creativity and the thought that it stimulates makes innovation more likely.

The more weak ties we have, the more connected to the world we are and are more likely to receive important information about ideas, threats and opportunities in time to respond to them.

Often our acquaintances' networks and our own networks have a very small intersection. Our weak ties know people we do not. This makes them very valuable during a career move.

Most of us have a lot of weak ties. All the people you've ever worked with, volunteered with, been part of professional organizations with, been neighbors with, stood on the sidelines of your kids' soccer games with—those are your weak ties. You might think you could never reach out to those people since they're virtually strangers. I'm here to tell you otherwise.

I was recently reintroduced to the "Strength of Weak Ties" concept through the book *Give and Take: Why Helping Others Drives Our Success* by Adam Grant.

Grant writes:

Mark Granovetter surveyed people in professional, technical, and managerial professions who recently changed jobs. Nearly 17 percent heard about the job from a strong tie. Their friends and trusted colleagues gave them plenty of leads.

By surprisingly people were significantly more likely to benefit from weak ties. Almost 28 percent heard about the job from a weak tie. Strong ties provide bonds, but weak ties served as bridges: they provide more efficient access to new information. Our strong ties tend to travel in the same social circles and know about the same opportunities as we do. Weak ties are more likely to open up access to a different network, facilitating the discovery of original leads.

Think about it. Everyone you've ever worked with or known has gone on to have new jobs, make new friends, create new business contacts. By such a calculation, your network is huge!

The only wrinkle is that it's tough to ask weak ties for help, for a lot of reasons. We're likely to feel embarrassed about asking anyone for help. Plus, when you reach out to weak ties there's a tendency to think:

- They're probably busy.

- I doubt they even remember me.

- This makes me look desperate.

One question you can ask yourself is: "What would I do if the shoe was on the other foot...if someone I had worked with reached out because they were looking to make a career change or had become unemployed?" You probably expect your weak ties to respond to you the way that you would respond to them. And you're probably right.

BE A GIVER

There are three kinds of people in the workplace: givers, takers, and matchers. The biggest point of the book *Give and Take* is that givers do prosper. And takers don't.

Givers are the kinds of people who are always looking for opportunities to help others, not because of what they will reap from the exchange, just because they have a worldview in which giving is inherently rewarding and appropriate. They do reap benefits in the long run, but that's a product of their giving, not the reason for it. These people are usually happy to help a former colleague, or anyone else for that matter.

Takers, on the other hand, are always self-interested. They are constantly looking for what they can get out of a relationship or exchange. They want to see how others can help them succeed and aren't thinking about how they can help others. These people would probably resent and ignore any demands on their time, like an email from an old colleague.

Then there are matchers ...

Matchers will give if they can see a personal or professional benefit arising from it. They give until they feel the balance has been tipped and they have given more than the other person or the team. Then they shift into self-protective mode.

156

Everything has to be "fair". These people will be happy to help you if they can ascertain that you can also be a benefit to them.

Matchers are the most common in our workplaces. If I help you, you will help me. If you help me, I will help you. Tit for tat. The lines between these styles are not hard and fast. You have probably worked with all three. One of the easiest places to spot differences is at a networking event. Takers go from person to person handing out their business cards and asking for yours. You get a LinkedIn connection request that evening, even though you barely talked with them. For them, it is a numbers game.

The differences between givers and matchers can be subtle. They are the ones who engage in the art of conversation. They want to learn more about you. A giver will usually end the conversation with the question, "How can I help you?"

If you recognize yourself as a taker, now is a good time to assess and change your behavior. What is your mindset when you interact with people? Is it to make a friend, see if you can help, or to quickly run through all the ways this person could help you? If that's the way you're thinking, you probably haven't built many bridges. Your first order of business might be to start looking for places to give: seek opportunities to volunteer, answer queries on social media threads about which you have expertise, offer to mentor or assist former colleagues or acquaintances who can benefit from your knowledge base.

If you're a giver it may be even more challenging for you to ask others for anything since you're used to being on the giving end. It's actually easier to give than it is to be the one who needs help. Think about how you'd like people to feel and respond to your giving, and humble yourself to walk in their shoes for a bit. Many people are probably delighted to have an opportunity to give back to you.

STEVE'S STORY

I spent a good bit of 2015 working with Steve, an introverted account manager. In the sales world, he was the "farmer." His job was to cultivate long-term relationships with his customers. Steve was really good at it.

Steve had spent over 20 years selling very specialized manufacturing equipment. One day, the company let go of over half of the sales staff. Steve was approaching 60 and he was scared. He had not searched for a job in decades and was afraid to tell anyone he was unemployed.

So, we started his process. We needed to dissect his personality using the Birkman Assessment and the Career Pivot evaluation process:

- What were his core needs at work?

- What made him feel valued?

- What energized and restored him? (Art and the outdoors.)

- What kind of boss did he want?

- How much structure did he need? (He was a structured anarchist!)

From the evaluation, we created a set of branding statements to work with and tackled his brand story. Together, we reworked his LinkedIn profile, connecting it to all of the complex products he sold in his previous position. We then developed a set of open-ended questions that he could use in any interview. He was now very prepared. He could explain why the right company should hire him. All of this was pretty standard for any job seeker. Then the real fun started.

Using LinkedIn, Steve reached out to colleagues he had worked with over the last 20-plus years. It was incredibly difficult for him to admit he was unemployed at this stage of his career. But he discovered that most of the people he reached out to had experienced unemployment in the last decade. We are long past the time when others assume that being unemployed means there is something wrong with *you*. The more Steve reached out to former colleagues, the easier it got. Steve is a really nice guy and a giver. He had built a lot of bridges and burned none. People remembered him and were willing to help.

HOW IT WORKS

Build a list of people you have worked with over the last 20 years. Divide this list into two:

- People who worked in the same function as you (HR, engineering, programming, sales, etc.)

- People who worked in a different function

Find your weak ties using LinkedIn search.

Use the Current Company or Past Company options to locate weak ties.

- For people who worked in the same function as you, see where they currently work. Did they change functional areas? If they did, reach out and ask them how they did it.

- For people who worked in a different function, what company and industry are they working in now? Have they changed industries? If they did, ask them how they did it.

In general, weak ties are easy to approach. Send them a personalized LinkedIn connection request that sounds something like this:

Jim,

We worked together at XYZ company in the mid-1990s. I am reaching out and reconnecting with former colleagues. If you are willing, I would like to schedule a short phone call with you to see how you are doing. In the meantime, please accept this invitation to connect.

Marc Miller

This is when you ask for AIR: Advice, Insights and Recommendations. Ask them for advice in your job search. Do they like working at their current employer? Can they recommend other companies that you should research? Will they introduce you to anyone at their current company or at another company?

When Steve did this, he was amazed by how many of his weak ties were delighted to hear from him. He was even more amazed by how many were willing to assist him in his job search. This greatly expanded his network and his visibility to companies and jobs. His weak ties proved to be invaluable. He found companies that needed account managers with his expertise.

Next, Steve harvested LinkedIn company pages. He started with his last employer and used the "similar companies" section to find companies that were either direct competitors or were in adjacent industries. After following this very deliberate process, he found the perfect match. A former colleague, and weak tie, worked for a company that made the component parts for the manufacturing equipment Steve previously sold. This company needed a national account manager!

The interviewing or, as I like to refer to it, the courting process, happened pretty quickly. It was only about six weeks from the time he was introduced to the company to the time he received an offer of employment.

Steve did not attend any networking events, which was his preference as an introvert. He spent all of his time researching his weak ties, reconnecting with them, and finding companies that were capable of hiring him. He did all of his "networking" one-on-one via email and phone conversations. He leveraged his network to the fullest. Steve had a network that was larger than he would ever have believed. Once he realized that just about everyone was willing to help, the whole process became a lot more comfortable. I told Steve early on that his next job would come through a relationship, and that he had no control over the timing. This is exactly what happened.

If you've had a career of any duration, make use of your weak ties. Whether for ideas, encouragement or connections, your extended network is probably a lot more powerful than you think. And when you talk to them, ask them if there is anything you can do to be a help to them. When you cultivate your giving tendencies all along the way, you develop a reputation in your extended network of being a giver. Plus, it's just a much nicer way to live.

ACTION STEPS

✓ Build a list of people you've worked with over the past 20 years. Begin to reach out to them over LinkedIn.

✓ Make sure you approach your search as a giver. If you haven't been a giver, look for opportunities to give. If you have been a giver, let someone else have the fun of giving this time!

✓ Use LinkedIn's Search to find people in similar functions and similar companies to the one you are interested in.

✓ Send these contacts a short note to see if they would be open to a call or coffee about positions in their company or industry. Ask for AIR!

For additional resources, check out the Repurpose Your Career Resource Center at CareerPivot.com/RYC-Resources

TIME TO ROLL UP YOUR SLEEVES

Let's face it: It would be great if we could snap our fingers and — Poof! — we have a new career, a better body, a fatter retirement account, and the ability to undo some of our history. While you can't undo your past, you can use what you've learned to make a better future.

Reviewing your past jobs, looking at what makes you happy, building a tribe — all these tasks take time. Whatever your personality, talents or temperament, you're going to run into something along the way that really challenges you. For me, it was asking for help. For some people, it might be taking on social media, facing a truth in their assessment, or just being on the bottom of the totem pole again. That's all right. Being challenged can be a good thing.

Creative destruction is not going to slow down but likely speed up. As new things are destroyed new opportunities are created which can either be terrifying or exciting. How you react to this new reality is your choice.

Don't give up. As we know, retirement at 65 is no longer a reality for most people. Many of you will work into your 70s and if you make the effort you will be working at something you enjoy.

You have decades ahead of you that you'll spend working. Isn't it worthwhile to invest some time now to create work you can enjoy? I know I'll probably be working the rest of my life. But I'd like that work to be something I enjoy and something I can spend fewer hours on than I used to spend at the office.

Be methodical. You can't make all these changes at once. Start with understanding yourself, your history, and your needs. Then work from there. If you want more help or guidance, check out the Repurpose Your Career Resource Center: CareerPivot.com/RYC-Resources/.

The Career Pivot Online Community is a place where you can join others on this journey. Check that out at CareerPivot.com/community

Make me part of your tribe!

Thanks for letting me share my journey with you. I wish you the best of everything in your search for a career that will grow with you!

ABOUT THE AUTHORS

Marc Miller has been recognized for having one of the top career blogs, top career sites, and top career podcasts in the U.S. by organizations including Forbes, Twitter, and Career Sherpa. He was named one of PBS's NextAvenue.org Influencers in Aging. *Repurpose Your Career* has been named one of the Best Career Development Books of All Time by Book Authority.

Marc's own career journey included 22 years at IBM, several thriving tech startups, painful stints as a high school teacher and as a fundraiser for the Jewish Community Association of Austin, and a near-fatal bicycle accident that changed his perspective forever.

Thirty years in the career desert taught him that most people build their careers without understanding what they actually need to be satisfied and fulfilled. They pursue money, status, a skill set, but find the happiness it brings them to be fleeting. They invest years of time and energy only to wind up feeling frustrated and trapped. Others have figured out what they need, but don't know how to chart a course to get there.

Marc found himself drawing on his own experiences to counsel friends and associates on their career journeys and realized he'd found his vocation. An active member of the Launchpad Job Club, he would use his extensive training experience to help others find careers that they could grow into for the decades that lie ahead, with all their promise of change.

Marc is passionate about his work and the clients he serves. He has taught in more than 35 countries and helped clients from many industries.

Marc and his wife now live in Ajijic Mexico where they can live a simpler and less expensive lifestyle but continue to support those in the 2nd half of life grow and thrive.

Susan Lahey grew up in the newsroom of *The Kansas City Star* and has freelanced for many publications on topics ranging from business and technology to art and sustainability. She has ghostwritten and co-written several books on personal development and finding and creating meaningful work.

Susan's own career has constantly evolved with the changes in journalism and digital content. In addition to writing on personal growth and evolution, she enjoys encouraging and mentoring others who are setting out on new paths. She has recently moved from Austin to Portugal.

Made in the USA
Columbia, SC
27 March 2023

14395938R10100